Andrew Jackson
and the Bank War

THE NORTON ESSAYS IN AMERICAN HISTORY
Under the general editorship of
HAROLD M. HYMAN
University of Illinois

EISENHOWER AND BERLIN, 1945: THE DECISION TO
HALT AT THE ELBE   *Stephen E. Ambrose*

THE MONEY QUESTION DURING RECONSTRUCTION
                                    Walter T. K. Nugent

ANDREW JACKSON AND THE BANK WAR
                                    Robert V. Remini

Andrew Jackson and the Bank War

A Study in the Growth of Presidential Power

Robert V. Remini

New York W · W · NORTON & COMPANY · INC ·

For Ruth

Contents

Preface

IN A RECENT BOOK, Walter W. Heller, former economic adviser to Presidents John F. Kennedy and Lyndon B. Johnson, advocated direct federal aid to individual states as one means of solving some of the nation's fiscal and administrative problems.* Mr. Heller correctly noted that his scheme was first employed by President Andrew Jackson toward the end of his administration when millions of dollars were awarded the states on a no-strings, unrestricted and unencumbered basis. The modern day relevance of this plan is yet to be determined. For his part, Jackson was forced into experimenting with money grants to the states because of his involvement in a larger conflict, namely his War against the Second Bank of the United States.

Although there are several books treating the Bank War, most of them emphasize the history of the Second Bank, biographical information of the leading contestants, or problems related to public finance or central banking. Of course, there are many ways of looking at the Bank War and it will always mean different things to different people. Someone has said it is like an octopus. Its tentacles are everywhere: in politics, in economics, in fiscal policy, in power struggles between individuals, classes and sections, and in social and ideological differences separating the major antagonists.

My purpose in writing this book was to slice off only one tentacle of the octopus, to restate the War as a political phenomenon. For, as I see it, that is essentially what the struggle was all about. Admittedly, there were many new forces at

* *New Dimensions of Political Economy* (Cambridge, 1966; also a Norton paperbound, 1967).

work in American society during the 1820s and 1830s reshaping the business community and creating hostility between the Bank on the one hand and rising capitalists, urban workers, and farmers on the other. But this book presumes to argue that the *destruction* of the Bank occurred because it got caught in a clash between two willful, proud, and stubborn men: Andrew Jackson and Nicholas Biddle. It was a battle involving arrogance, stupidity, and confusion. It was a clash that can be appreciated only by an understanding of the President's political psychology and only after an examination of the involved political events directly associated with the War.

Another reason for writing this extended account was the necessity, I felt, of emphasizing the ways in which the War transformed the presidential office: how Jackson capitalized on the struggle to strengthen the executive branch of the government and infuse it with much of the power it enjoys today. Jackson's reassessment of the character of the presidency as well as the nature of the relationship between his office and the people also deserve attention. These considerations are frequently overlooked when analyzing the long-range effects of the War, and to my mind are infinitely more important than questions such as whether central banking should or should not have been terminated in the 1830s.

There is a third reason. A few years ago I wrote a short biography of Jackson in which the chapter on the Bank War vigorously defended every aspect of the President's actions. Since writing that biography I have had an opportunity to pursue additional research and study. In the process I revised many ideas about the War and about Jackson's culpability in initiating and continuing the struggle. The invitation, therefore, to contribute a volume in this series offered an excellent opportunity to write a revised, more complete, and better balanced account of one of the most significant chapters in American history.

In the preparation of this work I am very grateful to the research board of the University of Illinois, Chicago Circle, for a grant-in-aid. I owe a great deal to my colleagues at the University, Professors Peter Coleman and Kenneth Lockridge, who read the entire manuscript and offered many valuable criticisms. Most of all, I am indebeted to Harold M. Hyman, the general editor of the Norton Essays in American History, who suggested numerous organizational changes in the text and waved many red flags each time Andrew Jackson threatened to get out of hand and dictate the direction of the story.

ROBERT V. REMINI

Evanston, Illinois

ABBREVIATIONS

In the interest of saving space, the following abbreviations have been used in the footnotes:

CHS	*Connecticut Historical Society*
CUL	*Columbia University Library*
HUL	*Harvard University Library*
LC	*Library of Congress*
MHS	*Massachusetts Historical Society*
ML	*Morgan Library, New York City*
NA	*National Archives*
NHHS	*New Hampshire Historical Society*
NYHS	*New York Historical Society*
NYPL	*New York Public Library*
NYSL	*New York State Library, Albany*
PHS	*Historical Society of Pennsylvania, Philadelphia*
PUL	*Princeton University Library*
TSL	*Tennessee State Library, Nashville*
UNCL	*University of North Carolina Library*
URL	*University of Rochester Library*

Andrew Jackson
and the Bank War

1

The Antagonists

THE BANK OF THE UNITED STATES, snorted President Andrew Jackson, was a "monster," a "hydra-headed" monster, a monster equipped with horns, hoofs, and tail and so dangerous that it impaired "the morals of our people," corrupted "our statesmen," and threatened "our liberty." It bought up "members of Congress by the Dozzen," he ranted, subverted the "electoral process," and sought "to destroy our republican institutions. . . ." Such a fearsome beast must not roam the country at will, he declared, at least not while Andrew Jackson sat in the White House. There was only one thing for him to do: kill the brute, and the sooner the better.[1]

Of course, Jackson was a wild romantic. He tended to represent all his enemies as devouring monsters threatening the lives of the American people. The Bank of the United States (BUS) was no exception and the President pursued it with all the vigor typical of his military and political campaigns. But he soon discovered that the BUS was unwilling to accept slaughter without a fight. It put up a struggle that was to last several years and give Jackson many anxious moments. When Martin Van Buren returned from Great Britain, where he had been United States Minister for a brief period, he came to see Jackson at the White House and was startled to find the old man lying on a couch looking very pale, almost ghostlike.

1. Jackson's extremely vivid descriptions of the Second Bank of the United States can be found in his many letters and official publications. See, for example, Jackson to William B. Lewis, April 29, 1833, Jackson-Lewis Papers, NYPL; James D. Richardson, *Messages and Papers of the Presidents* (Washington, 1897), II, 1304, 1224–1238; Amos Kendall to Jackson, March 20, 1833, Jackson Papers, LC.

As Van Buren walked into the room, the President glanced up, brightened, and reached out and grasped his friend's hand. "The bank, Mr. Van Buren, is trying to kill me," he said in a whisper. Then, pressing Van Buren's hand very tightly, he added, "but I will kill it." [2]

And that is precisely what Jackson did. At first he only intended to chain the beast to keep it from inflicting further harm, but he soon found himself locked in a death struggle with the monster. So, despite enormous problems that were certain to rise if the Bank were eliminated, despite intense opposition by large numbers of his party, despite strong arguments from intelligent and loyal friends about the senselessness of his action, Andrew Jackson destroyed the Second Bank of the United States. Reverberations from that clash echoed for over a hundred years.

Historians still argue about the meaning of the struggle and especially about the wisdom of obliterating this useful institution. To some the Bank War was an act of spite by an ignorant frontiersman whose stubbornness gravely injured his country.[3] To others the War marked the necessary termination of a privileged monopoly whose powers were so extensive that it could disrupt business and intimidate the government.[4] Before resolutions to these differences can be suggested, however, it is essential to take a closer look at the two antagonists and the circumstances that brought them to this momentous confrontation.

All his life Andrew Jackson was a fighter. Indeed, as a child and young man he was known as a wild roughneck, always into mischief, fighting, rollicking, getting into trouble. There was an air of restlessness about him, a tension that sometimes erupted in ugly acts of violence. Occasionally he bullied his friends, that is, if he got mad enough or if it suited his needs.

2. Martin Van Buren, *Autobiography* (Washington, 1920), 625.

3. For example, Thomas P. Govan, *Nicholas Biddle* (Chicago, 1959), 112ff.

4. For example, Arthur M. Schlesinger, Jr., *The Age of Jackson* (Boston, 1946), *passim*.

A story is told that as a boy he was playing with a gun one day when it accidentally discharged and floored him by its kick. Quickly, Jackson sprang to his feet and snarled at the boys standing around him: "By G-d, if one of you laughs, I'll kill him." And when Andrew Jackson spoke like that, few had the courage to call his bluff.[5]

Much of Jackson's wildness and disquiet as a youth can be attributed to a lack of parental guidance and supervision. Raised without a father, he was orphaned at the age of fourteen when his mother died of cholera while nursing American prisoners of war during the Revolution. His two brothers also died in the war and he himself was scarred on the forehead by a British officer's sword blow after he refused to clean the soldier's boots. When the Revolution ended, young Andrew drifted from one thing to another, finally landing in Salisbury, North Carolina, where he entered the law office of Spruce McCay and learned enough about the legal profession to be licensed an attorney. In 1788, at the age of twenty-one, he migrated westward to the country that eventually became Tennessee. By that time he was six-foot-one, cadaverously thin, with sharp features, intense blue eyes and bristling red hair that fell rakishly over his forehead and hid the scar inflicted on him during the Revolution.[6]

Jackson settled in Nashville where he became a successful lawyer, district attorney, and judge. He married Rachel Robertson Robards, whose family was among the original settlers of Nashville. As his law practice prospered, Jackson bought a small plantation on the Cumberland River for his home and continued to acquire enough land during the next several years to lay the foundations of a large estate. By the time Tennessee entered the Union as a state in 1796, he was an extensive landowner and socially a member of the upper class. "The secret of his prosperity," wrote an early biographer, "was that he acquired large tracts when large tracts could be bought for a horse or a cow bell, and held them till the torrent of emigration

5. James Parton, *The Life of Andrew Jackson* (New York, 1861), I, 64.

6. Robert V. Remini, *Andrew Jackson* (New York, 1966), 13–25.

made them valuable." [7]

But his land speculation eventually got him into difficulties that significantly shaped his future thinking about money and banks. In 1795 he journeyed to Philadelphia to sell 50,000 acres of land he held jointly with his friend, John Overton, and another 18,000 acres he had been commissioned to sell for a man named Joel Rice. After considerable trouble he found a buyer in David Allison, a Philadelphia merchant and speculator, who bought the lands at twenty cents per acre and gave promissory notes to cover the entire amount of the property. Planning to open a trading post on the Cumberland River in Tennessee, Jackson took his share of the money and purchased supplies from Meeker, Cochran and Company, turning over Allison's notes to the company to pay for the articles.

Then disaster struck. Allison went bankrupt in the fall of 1797. Meeker, Cochran and Company notified Jackson that Allison had defaulted and that he, Jackson, was responsible for the notes. Immediately, Jackson sold the store for 33,000 acres of land, and then sold the land for twenty-five cents an acre, accepting a draft for the money from William Blount, his long-time political mentor and supposedly a very rich man. Jackson hurried back to Philadelphia with the draft only to discover that Blount himself was involved with Allison and also caught in a financial squeeze. The situation was desperate, and it was only "with great difficulty," Jackson later recorded, that "[I] got up the paper I had endorsed, and was compelled in closing this disastrous business, to take D. Allisons paper for the amount [$20,000] due me. Thus David Allison became indebted to me. . . ." Ruefully, he added, "the land I sold . . . is now worth at least $200,000." [8]

Allison eventually died in debtor's prison. Before his death, however, he mortgaged 85,000 acres of Tennessee land to one Norton Pryor. Together, Pryor and Jackson brought suit against

7. Parton, *Jackson,* I, 157, 158, 172.

8. Jackson to James Jackson, August 25, 1819, Andrew Jackson, *Correspondence of Andrew Jackson* (Washington, 1927), II, 427. The Rice tract purchased by Jackson and Overton became the site on which the town of Memphis was founded. Jackson to Overton, June 18, 1795, Overton Papers, TSL.

Allison's heirs to gain clear title to the land, 5000 acres of which were earmarked for Jackson in payment of the $20,000 debt. Since Jackson was now a judge of the Superior Court of Tennessee and could not be involved in these legal proceedings, he prevailed upon John Overton to prosecute the case. Overton instituted suit in federal court and won, after which Jackson hastily sold the 5000 acres awarded him.

Several years later—either 1810 or 1811—Jackson was advised by his friend George W. Campbell that the decision obtained by Overton was invalid because a federal court lacked jurisdiction in such cases. "Having sold and made a general warrentee," wrote Jackson, "I became alarmed." For he instantly realized that he was liable to suit from those to whom he had sold the land—and not for its original price but for its current value.[9] As visions of financial ruin and debtor's prison raced through his mind, Jackson galloped off to Georgia where he understood the Allison heirs presently lived. He found the family and begged them to sign over to him "all their rights to any property within the state of Tennessee that they were invested with by descent as heirs of David Allison. . . ." Fortunately, he convinced them of his rights; they executed "a Deed to me," he wrote "and I executed to them a release against the [$20,000] debt." With the deed in hand he was able to give a clear title to those who bought the 5000 acres.[10]

Having come within an ace of total financial disaster, Jackson permanently altered his opinions about debts, paper (which is a promise to pay), and speculation. Thereafter he regarded land speculation as an abiding evil; he abhorred debts; and he referred to paper, whether offered by individuals or issued by banks, as the instrument of the swindler and the cheat. For Andrew Jackson, hard money—specie—was the only legitimate money; anything else was a fraud to steal from honest men.

Since banks did a great deal of speculating in land, for

9. *Ibid.*, 428.

10. *Ibid.* For various other aspects of the Allison deal see Jackson to Overton, June 9, 1795, Jackson, *Correspondence,* I, 14; Jackson to Lewis, July 16, Jackson-Lewis Papers, NYPL; the Jackson-Allison land deal, Jackson, *Correspondence,* I, 21, and Jackson to Overton, June 9, 1798, Overton Papers, TSL.

which they issued paper notes, Jackson also developed a deep
suspicion about banking practices. He observed that paper was
sometimes issued without the hard cash to cover it, and that
bank failures were not uncommon where speculation ran unchecked. Because he did not believe in credit—every man
should pay his debts just as he himself had—Jackson opposed
the note-issuing, credit-producing aspects of banking. Many
years later in a private conversation with Nicholas Biddle,
president of the Bank of the United States, Jackson told him
bluntly, "I do not dislike your bank any more than all banks.
But ever since I read the history of the South Sea Bubble I have
been afraid of banks." [11] The Bubble was a land speculation
in England by the South Sea Company that had ended in
financial disaster for thousands of people. It is possible that
this misadventure was a factor in Jackson's intense dislike of
banks; but more likely it was his own personal debacle that
forever prejudiced him against debts and paper money—and
against the people and institutions that manipulated them for
profit.

Jackson's prejudice was not the bias of a typical frontiersman
of his time. Paper and speculation, which he detested, were
heartily approved by many westerners. What worried most men
living near the frontier was that banks somehow or other made
money out of nothing, and that they always seemed to be doing
it for the benefit of "Easterners," "aristocrats," and "foreigners." Jackson absorbed some of this fear—several of his letters
refer to it—but it did not influence his thinking nearly as much
as the Allison affair. As for the United States Bank, Jackson admitted to an additional prejudice. Since he believed in states'
rights, he denied that the Constitution authorized the Bank's
establishment.

In 1804, in order to concentrate on his business affairs and
extricate himself from debt, Jackson resigned his judgeship. For
a time he returned to storekeeping, but a succession of bad
debts and other problems forced him out. Eventually, with the
help of his wife in managing his enterprises, he struggled back
to financial solvency, earning money from his law practice,

11. Biddle Memorandum, no date, Biddle Papers LC.

plantation, cotton gin, and horse breeding.[12] But his financial experiences left Jackson with very conservative ideas about finance, ideas still fixed in his mind when he entered the White House.

When war broke out in 1812, Jackson happened to be a major-general of the Tennessee militia, a circumstance that soon brought him fame and glory. He was a general not because of any military prowess he had demonstrated over the years, but because he had defeated all other prospective candidates in an election for the post. And a close election it was, too. By virtue of a single vote, cast by a political friend, Jackson was chosen general. No matter. He made a very good general. Sent against the Creek Nation in the South, he won a smashing victory and imposed a brutal treaty on the Indians that forever broke Creek power. But his greatest triumph occurred at New Orleans, where he repelled a British invasion and decimated their army just as the War of 1812 ended. Over 2000 of the enemy perished in the swamps, as against a dozen Americans. It was a victory that inflated national pride and fashioned Jackson into a hero for all time. During the Creek War his soldiers affectionately called him "Old Hickory" to indicate how tough he was; after New Orleans Americans saluted him as the "Old Hero," a man to whom the nation's debt was eternal.

In 1818, Jackson increased his fame by defeating the Seminole Indians and seizing Florida from the Spanish. Though his actions temporarily caused an international furor, it eventually led to the purchase of Florida by the United States. To help set up the administration of the newly-acquired territory, Jackson agreed to serve as governor, a post he held very briefly, though long enough to preside over the formal ouster of the Spanish and to establish local government in Florida.[13]

Jackson was fortunate to stride across the national scene at a time when the country was undergoing profound changes. By 1820 a new post-Revolutionary generation was pushing for-

12. Harriett S. Arnow, *Flowering of the Cumberland* (New York, 1963), 48–49.
13. For a colorful account of Jackson's military exploits see Marquis James, *Andrew Jackson, The Border Captain* (Indianapolis and New York, 1933), 141–249.

ward, anxious to seize power, leadership, and status from an older political, economic, and social elite. These "men on the make" found in Andrew Jackson a symbol of their own ambitions and hopes. Presumably, if an orphan boy from the pine woods of Carolina could make good, there was no reason why they, too, could not aspire to wealth and social status by relying on their own talents.

Soon politicians began to sense the response the General's popularity produced among the electorate and to realize how they might capitalize upon it in their own states and for their own goals. By 1828 they had erected an elaborate political organization called the Democratic party to reflect American demand. Astride that engine Old Hickory rode to the White House.[14]

Jackson was now sixty-one years old. Tall and slender, his face weathered and drawn, his jaw sharp and nearly jutting, he carried himself with military stiffness. His steely blue eyes instantly registered whatever passion boiled within his emaciated body. His stiff gray hair and long bony nose added to the appearance of a courageous, strong-willed soldier. But what his appearance did not show was the astute politician that Jackson had become over the years. Skillful and cautious in his handling of problems, he was a hard-headed political operator, deeply enamoured of power and driven by personal ambition.

Those who thought him ignorant, stubborn, and vindictive saw only one side of the man, although it was a side that truly existed, one dark and frightening. An extremely difficult person to get along with, he could be ruthless and arrogant, a bully and a tyrant. He judged men too quickly, and his judgments were frequently prejudiced by earlier assessments based on rumor or hearsay. Toward his enemies, his sense of justice was rigid and pitiless; toward his friends, lax and indulgent. If it served his purpose to frighten people, he faked temper tantrums, roaring at the top of his voice. He was perverse, too. If told he must do one thing, the chances were extremely good that he would do exactly the opposite. In some ways what was most disturbing of all was his passion for revenge.

14. Remini, *Jackson,* 91–105.

Whenever someone crossed him, he would go to heroic lengths to even accounts. On the two occasions of attempts against his life during his administration, he reacted by attacking his assailants and further exposing himself to danger. He did not instinctively back away to save his life, but charged forward, walking cane raised high, ready to strike back. After the first attack, he seemed more perturbed over the assassin's escape than the injuries he had sustained. "No villain has ever escaped me before," he thundered, "and he would not, had it not been for my confined situation." [15]

There was a brighter side to Jackson's character, however. Fiercely loyal to his friends and supporters, he could be courteous and understanding, compassionate and patient. If difficulties arose, he did not insist on his own way nor did he crack heads to force consent to his will. As Roger B. Taney correctly pointed out, Jackson "never felt the least dissatisfaction with any one of his Cabinet for opposing him or his most favorite measures, when the opposition was made openly and fairly and conducted with proper decorum." [16] But let opposition seem disingenuous or let it leak to the public and tarnish his reputation and the President became all fury and passion, a veritable demon, raging at those around him and swearing revenge.

As Jackson began his presidential term in 1829 some Americans had grave fears about what this uneducated, Indian-killing, hot-headed Westerner might do in office. But with all their fears and all their apprehension, they never imagined in their wildest dreams that he would destroy the United States Bank.

Like Jackson, the Bank of the United States had endured a troubled history. Alexander Hamilton, Secretary of the Treasury under George Washington, proposed it as part of an overall fiscal program to lift the country to its financial feet. As envisioned by Hamilton, a central fiscal system would be created by Congress' establishment of a parent bank in Philadelphia and

15. Parton, *Jackson,* III, 487.
16. Roger B. Taney, Bank War Manuscript, Taney Papers, LC.

branch banks located in the principal cities throughout the nation. This quasi-private banking network would serve as a depository for government funds as well as an agent for the collection of taxes; and it would issue bank notes, redeemable in specie and acceptable in the payment of taxes, thus increasing the supply of needed currency with which to finance the country's growth. The BUS would be chartered for twenty years, according to Hamilton's plan, with a capital stock of $10 million, four-fifths of which would be subscribed by private investors and one-fifth by the United States government. The management of the Bank would consist of a president and a board of directors elected by the stockholders; of the twenty-five board members, five would be appointed by the government.

A bill embodying these provisions squeezed through Congress early in 1791—but not without fierce controversy. Operation of the Bank by investors meant that the fiscal policy of the nation would be controlled, to a degree, by private citizens, most of them wealthy and northern. Although Hamilton was anxious to strengthen the bond between the government and the entrepreneurial classes, his purpose in proposing the Bank was not limited to the benefit of the well-to-do. He believed a national bank would unify and strengthen the country and provide it with sound and flexible credit and currency.

One of the most persistent arguments against the Bank—one James Madison articulated at length in the House of Representatives—contended that it lacked constitutional authorization. Consequently, when the bill chartering the BUS came to President Washington for his signature he hesitated; but, despite nagging doubts, he eventually signed the measure, accepting Hamilton's argument that the elastic clause of the Constitution provided the needed justification.

Once chartered, the First Bank of the United States roared off to an impressive start. Smart investors snapped up its stock and within a few days the price of the stock shot above par. Buyers were concentrated mainly in Boston, New York, Philadelphia, and Baltimore, but in a short time foreign investors bought whatever was available. With such an encouraging beginning, the American people readily accepted the Bank's notes, thereby rapidly increasing the supply of money.[17]

Although paper currency was essential to the country's settlement and industrialization, such leaders as Thomas Jefferson preferred specie, the gold and silver bimetallic system established by Congress in the Coinage Act of 1792. This act provided for "full-bodied" money, that is full-weight gold and silver coins whose commodity value equaled their exchange value. Congress declared these coins legal tender to be freely minted at the ratio of 15 to 1. Because the Coinage Act underrated the value of gold—a ratio of 15.5 to 1 would have been closer to the market value—it practically drove gold out of circulation as a medium of exchange. Not until Andrew Jackson's administration was the ratio changed to 16 to 1 in order to attract gold back into circulation, an action fully in accord with Old Hickory's monetary views. Ideally, if Jackson had his own way, he preferred a financial system in which the government placed its funds in a government treasury, dealt solely in gold and silver and demanded specie for the payment of taxes. Persuasive support for his conservative views came in 1833 with the publication of a popular book by a Philadelphia economist, William Gouge. The *Short History of Paper Money and Banking in the United States* not only projected an independent or sub-treasury system that allowed the government to divorce its funds from private banking but also advocated the retirement of bank notes of high denominations, thus replacing paper with specie in ordinary business transactions.

The bimetallic system that Jackson and other "hard-money" men advocated so intensely never worked efficiently. There were two reasons for this: first, as a consequence of the inaccurate appraisal in 1792 of the market ratio between gold and silver, and second, because specie had to compete with the less expensive and more readily available forms of bank-credit money that businessmen preferred. Thus a variety of paper circulated as money, most of it bank notes. These notes were

17. As used in this book, the term "money" is defined as both a unit of account and a medium of exchange. Paper money was sometimes called "rag money" or "funny money."

printed promises to pay in denominations as low as five cents and as high as $10,000.

Although the First Bank of the United States played a dominant role in swelling credit and currency facilities in the country, its charter was allowed to expire in 1811. What blocked Congressional action was the concerted opposition of nearly 100 state chartered banks, plus fear of foreign ownership of the Bank's stock and the old bugaboo about its unconstitutionality. As a result the country entered the War of 1812 without that valuable institution and nearly suffered financial catastrophe. Specie virtually disappeared from circulation. Bartenders, barbers, innkeepers, and others issued fractional paper money in order to operate their businesses, prices rose more than 100 per cent, and the government was forced to act as its own tax collector. These developments plus the unchecked inflation created during the war by the vast amount of notes issued by state-chartered private banks convinced President James Madison to sign a bill on May 10, 1816, creating the Second Bank of the United States.

The new charter established the Bank for twenty years; raised its capital stock to $35 million—a whopping three-and-a-half times what it had been with the First Bank—shared on a four-fifths to one-fifth basis between the government and the public; authorized the creation of branch banks; [18] and ap-

18. Almost immediately the Second Bank of the United States established eighteen branches: Augusta, Georgia, opened and closed in 1817; Baltimore, opened in 1817; Boston, opened in 1817; Charleston, South Carolina, opened in 1817; Chillicothe, Ohio, opened in 1817 and closed in 1825; Cincinnati, Ohio, opened in 1817, closed in 1820 and reopened in 1825; Fayetteville, North Carolina, opened in 1817; Lexington, Kentucky, opened in 1817; Louisville, Kentucky, opened in 1817; Middletown, Connecticut, opened in 1817 and moved to Hartford in 1824; New Orleans, opened in 1817; New York City, opened in 1817; Norfolk, Virginia, opened in 1817; Pittsburgh, opened in 1817; Portsmouth, New Hampshire, opened in 1817; Providence, Rhode Island, opened in 1817; Richmond, Virginia, opened in 1817; Savannah, Georgia, opened in 1817; and Washington, D.C., opened in 1817. For the next several years no new branches were established. Then, in 1826, the branch in Mobile, Alabama, opened; in 1827, the branch in Nashville, Tennessee, opened; in 1828, the branch in Portland, Maine, opened; in 1829, the branch in Buffalo, New York opened; in 1829, the branch in St. Louis, Missouri, opened; in 1830, the branch in Burlington, Vermont, opened; in 1830, the branch in Utica,

proved the issuance of notes in denominations no smaller than five dollars. Many of the features of the new Bank resembled those of the old, except that the government received a bonus of $1.5 million for granting the charter, payable in three installments during the first years of the Bank's operation. And, as it had in the past, the Bank served as a depository for the Treasury and was subject to Treasury inspection.[19]

The first president of the Second Bank was Captain William Jones, onetime Secretary of the Navy and Secretary *pro tem* of the Treasury. He was a political choice—Madison's own—and a worse one would have been impossible to imagine. Ignorant and venal, Jones had just gone through bankruptcy. As president of the new Bank he quickly proved that the bankruptcy was no accident, for his actions nearly ruined the BUS during the first year of its operation. To begin with, he speculated in the Bank's stock, as did many of the branch managers; in addition, he permitted state banks to over-trade and inflate the currency to the point of precipitating a panic; also, he profited financially from the crooked operations of the Baltimore branch; and he repeatedly violated the terms of the charter as though the law were inoperative.[20] When Congress finally called an investigation, the stock of the BUS dropped below par which forced Jones into submitting his resignation. He was replaced as president in 1819 by Langdon Cheves of South Carolina, a former Congressman and Speaker of the House of Representatives.

Cheves soon put the Bank to rights. But his method was an agony. In effect he tied the country to a rack and gingerly turned the stretching wheel. To restore the Bank to financial soundness, loans were called in and mortgages were foreclosed. The notes of state banks in all parts of the country were

---

New York, opened; and in 1830, the branch in Natchez, Mississippi, opened.

19. Ralph C. H. Catterall, *The Second Bank of the United States* (Chicago, 1903), 10–21.

20. *Ibid.*, 30–49; Leon M. Schur, "The Second Bank of the United States and the Inflation After the War of 1812," *The Journal of Political Economy* (April, 1960), LXVIII, 118; Bray Hammond, *Banks and Politics in America* (Princeton, 1957), 258.

gathered and presented for payment—in specie. Since many of these banks had overspeculated through the encouragement of the BUS and were without gold or silver, they could not meet their obligations and so slid into bankruptcy, ruining many investors at the same time. The resulting depression brought a price collapse, unemployment, and, in some areas, starvation. Although this Panic was part of a worldwide shock, it was precipitated in the United States by the actions of the Bank, actions stemming from its own mismanagement.[21]

The people, in their distress, turned on the Bank. "All the evils which the community in particular parts of the country has suffered from the sudden decrease of the currency, as well as from its depreciation," wrote William H. Crawford, Secretary of the Treasury, "have been ascribed to the Bank of the United States." [22] The anger soon seeped into the law when several states enacted statutes aimed at penalizing the BUS. Six states heavily taxed branches of the Bank, and fourteen passed stay laws to prevent the Bank from collecting its debts. The resentment was particularly evident in the West where political repercussions reverberated for almost ten years.[23]

In Kentucky, for example, the legislature rushed to the relief of its people by enacting stay laws to prevent foreclosures, abolishing imprisonment for debt and chartering the Bank of the Commonwealth with permission to issue $3 million worth of paper. These radical measures produced violent internal reactions and split the Kentucky Republican party into two opposing factions: the Relief party and the Anti-Relief party. The Anti-Relief party, composed of merchants, large farmers, and lawyers, brought suit against the new laws and won their case before the Court of Appeals, Kentucky's highest court. Immediately, the Relief party, made up of small farmers,

21. Leon Schur states that the Bank's policy of curtailment precipitated the depression but did not cause it. Schur, "Second Bank and the Inflation," *Journal of Political Economy*, LXVIII, 134. See also Murray N. Rothbard, *The Panic of 1819* (New York, 1962), 13.

22. *American State Papers*, Finance, III, 508.

23. Walter B. Smith, *Economic Aspects of the Second Bank of the United States* (Cambridge, Massachusetts, 1953), 117–127; Robert V. Remini, *The Election of Andrew Jackson* (New York, 1963), 148.

debtors, and lawyers, won control of the legislature, abolished
the Court of Appeals, and created a New Court. The chief justice
of the New Court was William T. Barry, later postmaster general
under President Jackson, while the clerk of the New Court was
Francis Preston Blair, later an officer of the Commonwealth
Bank.

Blair was also an associate of Amos Kendall, editor of the
Kentucky *Argus of Western America* and one of the more
articulate leaders of the Relief party. Kendall had criticized the
management of the BUS since 1818 and for his efforts had been
labelled a "political incendiary" determined to "produce civil
commotion" and guilty of "a base and open endeavor to excite
actual warfare between the State of Kentucky and the Government of the United States." [24] Kendall never got over his spite
against the Bank and together with Blair he produced more
than a "civil commotion." These two incendiaries were quite
a sight. Kendall was an awkward and homely man, whose
sallow complexion was accentuated by his prematurely white
hair. Nearsighted, stooped, and chronically ill, he seemed
perpetually enveloped in a profound silence. But when he
picked up his editorial pen this "quiet man" was suddenly
transformed into a screaming banshee, producing sounds so
terrifying as to paralyze his enemies with fright. His associate,
Blair, was another strange-looking man. Small, mousy, weigh-
ing hardly a hundred pounds, he made up in journalistic
strength what he lacked in physical size. And these two gro-
tesques worked like demons for Jackson in the presidential
election of 1828, helping to win votes from all factions within
Kentucky. As a reward, Jackson appointed Kendall the fourth
auditor to the Treasury, and in 1830 brought Blair to Washington to edit the *Globe*. Both men were close advisers to the
President, and both carried to Washington a ferocious hatred
for the Second Bank of the United States.[25]

24. Amos Kendall, *Autobiography* (New York, 1949), 206–207.
25. Kendall said he and Blair had been opposed to the BUS since
1817. Kendall, *Autobiography*, 375. Earl G. Swen, ed., *Letters on Conditions in Kentucky 1825*, 12–23; W. W. Worsley to Henry Clay, November
3, 1826, Henry Clay Papers, LC; Hammond, *Banks and Politics*, 325, 332–
334; Schlesinger, *Age of Jackson*, 67–72.

In Tennessee, resentment against the BUS took another form. When the arbitrary conduct of two state banks in Nashville and Knoxville brought attempts by some leading merchants to have a branch of the Second Bank established in the state, the legislature blocked the action by levying a $50,000 tax on any bank chartered outside the state.[26] Andrew Jackson approved the tax, calling the attempted establishment of a branch the action of "the arristocratic few in Nashville." [27] Several years later, however, efforts were renewed to bring the BUS to Tennessee by repealing the $50,000 tax. As soon as he heard of the "secrete and combined movement of the arristocracy" to eliminate the tax, Jackson rushed to Nashville, summoned Robert C. Foster, the House Speaker, and "expostulated with him upon the danger of repealing the law." Jackson argued "that the intention was to introduce a branch of the united states Bank which would drain the state of its specie to the amount of its profits for the support and prosperity of other places, and the Lords, Dukes and Ladies of foreign countries who held the greater part of its stock." [28] His arguments got nowhere. The tax was eventually repealed, and not much later the BUS was petitioned by Nashville merchants to establish a branch in Tennessee. Because he was a prominent man in the community, Jackson was asked to sign the petition. He indignantly and vehemently refused, a reaction the merchants expected but which they shrugged off, convinced they would get the branch with or without his help.

Before final action was taken on this petition, General Thomas Cadwalader, a director of the BUS, came to Nashville and dined with Jackson. But this gesture of good will did not soften the Old Hero's opposition. "I have been opposed always to the Bank of the u.s.," he later wrote, "as well as all state Banks of paper issues, upon constitutional grounds believing as I do, that the congress has no constitutional power to grant a charter and the states are prohibited from granting charters of

26. Hugh Lawson White, president of the Knoxville bank and also a member of the legislature, was instrumental in getting the tax passed.

27. Jackson to Thomas Hart Benton, no date, Jackson Papers, LC.

28. *Ibid.*

paper issues." [29] Nevertheless, as a final attempt to win his approbation, the Bank asked him to write letters of recommendation for the candidates for president and cashier of the proposed Nashville branch. Jackson did so, believing the two men suggested for the posts to be "honest and fit and would direct the institution well and as far as they had control would not wield it to corrupt political principles." So the branch came to Nashville, much to Jackson's disgust. The people, he fumed, would be "cursed with all [the bank's] attendant evils and corruption." [30]

Like Tennessee, other states used their taxing power either to keep the hated Bank from crossing their borders or else to get rid of it after it had nudged its way in. Maryland, for example, imposed a tax on the Baltimore branch in 1818, and was immediately sued by the Bank. The branch lost its case in the state courts, but appealed to the United States Supreme Court for a reversal of the judgment. In the action *McCulloch* v. *Maryland,* Chief Justice John Marshall found in favor of the BUS. He denied that the states had the right to tax an agency of the federal government, declaring that "the power to tax involves the power to destroy." Also, Marshall, turning to the old problem of Congress' right to establish a national bank, a question still sharply debated in many states, agreed with the Hamiltonian contention that Congress possessed implied powers to carry out its enumerated responsibilities as well as powers that were "necessary and proper" to accomplish a legitimate end within the scope of the Constitution.[31]

Westerners furiously protested the McCulloch decision. There were threats against the Court and calls for constitutional amendments to overturn the decision. In Ohio, where the BUS was faulted for the state's financial problems, the state's auditor, Ralph Osborn, disregarded the McCulloch decision and demanded that the Bank pay the $50,000 tax already imposed. The Bank refused and obtained an injunction from a federal

29. *Ibid.*

30. *Ibid.* Charles G. Sellers, Jr., "Banking and Politics in Jackson's Tennessee, 1817–1827," *Mississippi Valley Historical Review* (June, 1954), XLI, 61–84.

31. 4 Wheaton 316ff.

circuit court restraining Osborn. The auditor ignored the injunc-
tion and when the tax was again refused, he seized the Bank's
specie and paper. Suit was brought against him and other state
officials involved in the seizure, whereupon the legislature
ordered the Bank out of Ohio.

In 1824 the case *Osborn* v. *the Bank of the United States*
reached the Supreme Court and, as anticipated, Marshall declared in the Bank's favor. Furthermore, he ruled that an agent
of the state—in this case, Osborn—when acting under the authority of an unconstitutional law was personally responsible
for damages resulting from his attempts to enforce the law.[32]

Thus, in the 1820's, partly due to its own mistakes and partly
due to circumstances it could not control, the Bank of the
United States had earned widespread hatred and fear throughout a substantial part of the nation. However, this animosity
abated considerably when Langdon Cheves resigned as President of the Bank and Nicholas Biddle replaced him. Under
Biddle's wise leadership the Bank became a valuable ally to
business just as the country moved into a new period of expansion and economic thrust. Providing the necessary capital for
this expansion, the Bank helped to advance a decade of hitherto
unparalleled prosperity.

At the time of his election to the presidency of the Bank,
Nicholas Biddle was thirty-seven years old and the pride of a
distinguished and well-to-do Philadelphia family. He had
everything: looks, brains, money, family, taste, and intel-
lectual and literary interests. He was born in 1786, the son of
Charles Biddle, a successful merchant who had served in the
Revolution and had become vice president of the Supreme
Executive Council of Pennsylvania. Nicholas Biddle entered
the University of Pennsylvania at the age of ten and completed
all the requirements for a degree within three years, but because of his extreme youth, the University refused to grant him
his diploma. So he entered Princeton, and in 1801, at the age
of 15, received his baccalaureate as valedictorian of his class.
Not much later, he made the grand tour of Europe, finding
Greece a land of such incomparable beauty that he became a

32. 9 Wheaton 738ff.

lifelong advocate of the restoration of classical art and architecture. In London, where he served as temporary secretary to James Monroe, the American Minister to Great Britain, he discoursed so well on ancient Greece before an audience of Cambridge scholars that Monroe could scarcely repress "his exultation and delight." [33] Having won a powerful friend in Monroe, a friendship that would later change the course of his life, and having satisfied his delight in European culture, Biddle returned to the United States in 1807 and took up the practice of law. He was elected to the lower house of the Pennsylvania legislature in 1810, the same year that his father was elected to the upper house. Then, to crown his achievements, he married an heiress, Jane Craig, the daughter of one of Philadelphia's wealthiest men. In addition to everything else, his marriage brought ownership of a country estate, called "Andalusia," where Biddle was able to indulge his taste for Grecian beauty.

While serving in the Pennsylvania legislature Biddle acquired a sophisticated understanding of the operation of the Bank of the United States. Not that he was interested in banks *per se*; rather he was fascinated in them as a "function of the economy." [34] Later, when Biddle failed to win election to Congress, James Monroe, now President of the United States, appointed him to the Bank's board of directors. Rapidly sponging up knowledge about the business of the BUS, he soon gained a reputation as the most articulate, brightest, and best-informed member of the board. Thus, when Cheves resigned as president, Biddle was the obvious choice to succeed him. Not only was he a Philadelphian (and this was important because of the parent Bank's location), but he was a friend of President Monroe (also important) and had demonstrated marked business acumen (not quite as important).[35] So, on January 7, 1823, Nicholas Biddle was elevated to the exalted position of President of the United States Bank.

In appearance, he was strikingly handsome. His oval face

33. Quoted in Govan, *Biddle,* 20.
34. Hammond, *Banks and Politics,* 291.
35. Fritz Redlich, *The Moulding of American Banking* (New York, 1947), I, 113.

with its high forehead, straight nose, and round chin was framed
in long chestnut-colored hair lying in close curls around his head.
Standing five-feet seven-inches tall, he was fair-complexioned
and rather romantic looking, though not effeminate. His bearing
was distinctly aristocratic. Withal there was the appearance of
a sensitive, intelligent, cultivated man, more like a misty-eyed
poet than a sharp-nosed banker. For Biddle was not a crass,
money-grubbing stock-jobber like so many of his contemporaries. He was a man of affairs, highly educated and urbane,
who could bring "liberal habits of thinking" to the Bank's
operations.[36] Strong willed and energetic, he was quick to catch
a point and even quicker to act on it. John Quincy Adams said
he was a man anyone would be "justly proud to call his friend;
a man of eminent ability, of a highly cultivated mind, of an
equable and placid temper, and in every other relation of life,
of integrity irreproachable and unreproached. . . ." [37] Considering the source—the hyper-critical Adams—this was praise
indeed.

Still, Biddle had his faults. Before anything else, he was
arrogant. Impossibly arrogant. And vain. Moreover, there
was a lot that was counterfeit in Biddle. He pretended to be an
expert in many things when all along he only seemed to be an
expert, which was what he really cared about. Appearance
was all. It has been said that Biddle was too fond of playing
and looking like a banker instead of being one. When problems
arose within the BUS, instead of confronting them, he instinctively covered them up. Rather than attack the difficulties,
he tended to "smooth things over and present a good face in
spite of facts." [38] This sense of insecurity, if that is what it was,
prompted him to offer excuses or denials whenever the management of any branch was criticized. Inordinately sensitive
about the Bank's operations, he frequently defended the unsup-
portable when it would have been infinitely better to admit
the faults and then correct them. On several occasions he
was to exasperate President Jackson by his repeated refusal to

36. Smith, *Economic Aspects,* 14.
37. Quoted in *ibid.,* 15.
38. William G. Sumner, *Andrew Jackson* (Boston and New York,
1882), 312–313.

investigate fairly the many accusations of mismanagement in several of the branch banks.

There also have been questions about Biddle's personal integrity. Not that he regularly slipped his hand into the till to mount another Grecian urn at Andalusia. Nothing so obvious. But those who have examined his papers and studied the history of the Bank frequently come away with a "very disagreeable sense of suspicion," [39] as though Biddle had used the Bank to serve purposes outside the limitations of the charter. For example, he was not above extending the Bank's money to its friends and refusing loans to those considered unfriendly. The favoritism he showed toward Daniel Webster and one or two other privileged Congressmen unnecessarily exposed the BUS to devastating public criticism.

Yet, with all his limitations, it must be said that Biddle was the best thing that ever happened to the Bank. He was a brilliant administrator, the prototype of the modern business executive, who had a genuine comprehension of the subtleties of banking. Most important of all, by his energy, aggressiveness, and intelligence, he transformed what was essentially a nationwide branch-banking system, acting as a federal fiscal agent, into a bona-fide central bank.[40]

To avoid confusion and misunderstanding, certain definitions and explanations of banking terms are imperative at this point. Commercial banks are here defined as profit-seeking, privately owned institutions which create cash deposits payable in legal tender on demand. The term "central bank" is defined as an institution acting as an agent of the federal government that creates and destroys the circulating media. It normally exercised this control of the media through its influence on the reserves (specie and paper) of commercial banks. To do this, it simply varied its holding of the outstanding notes issued by the commercial banks. It restrained these banks by presenting their notes to them for redemption in specie. This action automatically contracted the specie and credit of the affected banks.

39. *Ibid.,* 313.
40. Redlich, *Moulding of American Banking,* 113, 118; Jacob Meerman, "The Climax of the Bank War: Biddle's Contraction, 1833–34," *Journal of Political Economy* (August, 1963), LXXI, 379.

Conversely, a central bank permitted commercial banks to expand their credit by buying and holding the notes or paying them out under normal business conditions. Several factors gave the BUS its special advantages to assume the functions of a central bank: it had enormous reserves provided by the government; its own notes were legal tender for all debts owed by or payable to the government; and as the depository of the government, it received the notes of other banks and thus became their creditor.

Most importantly, the BUS had a powerful lever on state banks, which it achieved by acquiring their notes. This acquisition took two principal forms: since the BUS managed (but did not own) the federal tax revenues deposited with it and since these taxes were frequently offered in the form of state bank notes, the Bank could either accept and hold the notes or it could present them to the issuing banks and demand specie; further, since the BUS had tremendous resources of its own, it could go into the money market and buy state banknotes and then present them for redemption to the issuing banks.

The state banks were state-chartered, commercial enterprises. Because their reserves were limited, their financial success depended in large measure on their ability to keep their notes in circulation. Otherwise they had to rely solely on the assets of their stockholders and depositors. A bank counted itself very lucky—indeed it was a banker's dream come true— if its notes were never returned for redemption. This explains why banks fought to keep the notes of their competitors out of circulation and why existing banks brought political pressure to prevent the chartering of new banks or the renewal of expired charters for existing banks.

Obviously, notes of small denominations tended to remain in circulation for a long period of time, while large notes were quickly returned for redemption. In the early period of American banking, state banks issued many small-denomination notes. They also dealt mainly in short-term loans involving commercial enterprises. After 1800, they issued much larger notes and resorted to long-term loans to accommodate the needs of farmers and manufacturers who required extended credit.

These commercial banking functions were also performed by the Bank of the United States which accepted deposits and made loans to the public. When Biddle became president, he managed the institution as both a commercial and central bank. Upon election, he outlined his general policy: "The view which I have of the true policy of the Bank is this. . . . To bank where there is some use and some profit in it, and therefore . . . to make at present the larger commercial cities the principal scene of our operations." [41] He also encouraged short-term commercial loans, and he required prompt and full payment of debts from state banks. He limited the redeemability of the Bank's notes by directing that all notes above five dollars could be redeemed at par only at the branch of issue and at Philadelphia, which tended to increase the circulation of the Bank's notes.[42] Eventually he succeeded in providing the South and West with stable paper money by encouraging the branches in those areas to make loans on bills of exchange payable in the East. And, to a large extent, this action helped to wipe out lingering animosity toward the BUS. But perhaps Biddle's greatest success was the issuance of the branch drafts, a device by which he suppressed the depreciated currencies of the West and South, increased the currency by about one-fourth, and provided the country with a relatively safe and uniform currency.

State banks, in issuing their notes, provided a valuable means of creating capital to finance the industrialization of the country. Because of the importance of these notes and in order to prevent them from being driven from circulation by the BUS, the Congress, in chartering the Bank, required that its notes be signed by its president and countersigned by its cashier. These officers clearly did not have the time or the physical stamina to sign enough small notes to satisfy all the branches with the currency they needed. While there were

41. Biddle to Robert Lenox, February 3, 1823, Biddle Papers, LC.
42. Notes of $5 were redeemable at all branches. These constituted ⅙th of the Bank's note issue.

sufficiently large denomination notes in circulation for use in business, there were not enough small denomination notes to pass as currency. In this way, the notes of the small banks were protected.

Biddle was severely hampered in his financial operations by this requirement. Repeatedly, the BUS asked Congress to change the law, and repeatedly the Congress refused. So Biddle conceived the branch drafts as a way of getting around the law. He convinced his board of directors (after first getting a legal opinion from Daniel Webster and Horace Binney, both of whom were members of the board) to allow him to authorize the issuance of five- and ten-dollar drafts by all the branches after they were signed by the branch presidents and cashiers. The drafts were prepared in blank at Philadelphia and distributed to the branches, whereupon the branches endorsed the drafts "payable to bearer" and issued them according to their needs. Since the drafts were made to look like bank notes in design, color, and texture—so that few could tell the difference—and since they were acceptable in payment of taxes owed the government, these drafts readily passed as money. Later, Biddle printed twenty-dollar drafts and kept them in circulation by issuing them on branches in remote cities where it was virtually impossible to take them for redemption in specie. By 1832 the Bank had printed over $11 million of these drafts, although their net circulation came to just over $5 million.[43]

By the use of these branch drafts, Biddle struck at the business of the state banks. For, at the same time he floated his drafts, he also presented the paper of the state banks for immediate redemption in specie. This double-action speedily drove the depreciated currencies from circulation. Biddle hit hardest in the West and South where inflationary tendencies had been the greatest. The practice was a bit ruthless and clearly in defiance of the known will of Congress, but as the friends of the Bank frequently explained, it succeeded in providing the nation with sound and ample currency, one eminently suitable to the expanding needs of the economy.

43. Catterall, *Second Bank,* 114, 119, 129.

Thus, under Biddle, the Bank prospered. It branched into twenty-nine cities from its headquarters on Chestnut Street in Philadelphia (in a structure built in 1824 and designed—naturally—to look like a Greek temple), doing a business of $70 million a year. It was a remarkably efficient central-banking system, not simply a branch-banking system acting as a tax collector for the U.S. Treasury. It handled 20 per cent of the country's loans; its note circulation came to $21 million, which was about one-fifth of the nation's total; and it held one-third of the total bank deposits and specie.[44] But these numbers do not tell a complete story, for the Bank's influence and strength went far beyond the limitations suggested by these figures. By 1828 the Bank was a financial colossus, entrenched in the nation's economy, possessing the means of draining specie from state banks at will and regulating the currency according to its own estimate of the nation's needs.

As long as the financial operations in the country functioned smoothly and efficiently, the Bank did not misuse its massive power. Because of its turbulent history it was now seeking a benign image. And, because of its conscious effort to erase the past, much of the earlier animosity disappeared by the end of the 1820's. Still the past was not completely wiped out, so that when President Andrew Jackson summoned popular support for his War against the Bank, men from all classes joined him in the fight. Furthermore, they represented every section of the country. Undoubtedly the first and largest anti-Bank group to answer the President's call was the mass of voters who agreed with Jackson that the Bank, because of its money and power, threatened the safety of the Republic. A second group included those seeking economic advantage who felt they had been denied this advantage by the actions of the central bank. Still a third group included state bankers and their stockholders who had experienced the power of the BUS and resented its size, wealth, and controlling influence. This resentment would apply to Wall Street bankers as well as to small-town bankers. Commercial and manufacturing groups

44. Glyndon G. Van Deusen, *The Jacksonian Era* (New York, 1959), 63.

and ambitious professionals of all kinds who collided with the
Bank's restrictive credit policies also joined Jackson, as did
those urban wage earners who viewed the Bank as the largest
among many monopolies equipped with special privileges to
grind the faces of the poor. Finally, there were freeholding farmers who regarded the BUS as the embodiment of all the corrupting forces in society threatening their simple republican way of
life.

Westerners and Southerners harbored a decade-old prejudice
against the Bank, while strict constructionists, no matter what
their geographical origin, condemned the Bank as an unconstitutional extension of the authority of the central government.
Those jealous of the power accruing to Philadelphia because of
the Bank's presence on Chestnut Street had an itch to topple
the Greek Temple; and there was a small army of lawyers and
politicians who reckoned some gain by doing Jackson's bidding.
In short, the Bank's enemies were a diverse group from all
walks of life and from every section of the country. But most of
them had one thing in common: they were aggressive, both
politically and economically, and not unwilling to use their
strength or influence to destroy what stood in their way.[45]

If the Bank had incurred such widespread enmity from so
many classes—hardly one is omitted—who, then, were its
friends, and how many of them were there? Probably the
only sensible answer to this question (although it sounds like
a hedge) is to say that support came from all classes and
groups—but particularly from the upper classes. (Of course there
were some Americans who were supremely indifferent to the
issue and whose animosity or loyalty could not be roused by
any amount of party rhetoric.) But certainly there were many
men from every section of the country, including the West and
South, who benefited directly from the operations of the BUS

45. An analysis of the various classes and groups opposing the Bank
can be found in Schlesinger, *Age of Jackson,* Marvin Meyers, *The Jacksonian Persuasion* (Stanford, 1957), Richard Hofstadter, *The American
Political Tradition* (New York, 1948), Frederick Jackson Turner, *Rise of
the New West* (New York, 1935), Catterall, *Second Bank,* Bray Hammond, *Banks and Politics,* and Louis Hartz, *The Liberal Tradition in
America* (New York, 1955).

and who appreciated its value as a central bank, both for themselves and their communities. Indeed, it is very possible that a *substantial majority* of Americans approved the Bank, favored its recharter, and opposed Jackson's removal of the government's deposits from the Bank in 1833! If this is true, then the magnitude of Old Hickory's accomplishment in destroying the BUS becomes even more impressive.

Statistical evidence to prove overwhelming popular support for the Bank is by no means conclusive. However, a degree of evidence exists to lend credence to the thesis. No nationwide public opinion polls were taken, but where individuals were asked to sign petitions to Congress favoring or disapproving the Bank, the preponderant majority of those who signed them approved the BUS.[46] When the question of recharter first came up in Congress, over one hundred memorials flooded into Washington supporting recharter. But less than a dozen were received opposing recharter.[47] When Jackson removed the deposits from the BUS the number of resolutions more than doubled. During the 1833–34 congressional session, the Senate received exactly 243 memorials favoring the restoration of the deposits and the rechartering of the Bank. These memorials were signed by 128,117 individuals. During the same period only 55 resolutions were received opposing the restoration of the deposits, signed by a total of 17,027 men. And of these 55 resolutions, 40 of them came from three highly organized Democratic states: Pennsylvania (17 resolutions), New York (13), and New Jersey (10). Only one came from a Western state—Ohio.[48]

It can be argued, of course, that the great disparity in the number of people who signed petitions is attributable to the skill of Biddle in organizing (and perhaps paying for) this

46. These do not include memorials from state banks, however.

47. *Executive Documents* (House) 22nd Congress, 1st Session, Vol. III, document 92; Vol. IV, documents 111, 108, 119, 142, 141, 139, 136, 157, 150, 159, 168, 165, 107; Vol. V, document 192. Unfortunately many of these memorials do not carry the names of the individual petitioners, but where they do, the number of names in favor of the Bank average from 400 to 500, while those opposed to the Bank average a dozen or less.

48. *Senate Documents,* 23rd Congress, 1st Session, Vol. VI, document 459.

demonstration of support. However, the Jacksonians were not exactly amateurs when it came to organization; nor were they naive about the value and necessity of creating the appearance of mass support. And it must be noted that the difference in the figures was extremely impressive: over 128,000 pro-Bank signatures as against 17,000 anti-Bank signatures. At the same time these petitions were reaching Congress, Jackson himself was busy urging party leaders to "Get up meetings and memorials" against the BUS.[49] Obviously, the leaders could not oblige him, at least not in the case of the memorials. So it is very unlikely that the tremendous number of signers favoring the Bank (and the comparatively small number opposing the BUS) was the result primarily of the enterprise of Biddle or the lack of it by Democrats.

Unfortunately, there are not many recorded instances where people were given a choice of signing a petition either for or against the Bank, for or against recharter. But on the rare occasions when they were given this choice those men favoring the BUS outnumbered those opposed by more than 5 to 1.[50] To this inconclusive statistical documentation may be added the impressionistic evidence gathered from reading the correspondence of a number of Congressmen. The impression, again inconclusive, is that Congressional mail ran strongly in favor of the Bank.

If it is possible that most Americans favored the Bank, how then was it destroyed? And who was responsible? Curiously, some historians have had trouble identifying the "culprit." It is not enough for them to say "Andrew Jackson" and be done with it. They prefer to see hidden conspiracies involving all sorts of unlovely characters, from Wall Street bankers and conniving politicians in Albany, to such White House schemers as Amos Kendall, Isaac Hill, Roger B. Taney, Francis P. Blair, and others.[51] But the evidence is overwhelm-

49. Jackson to Van Buren, January 3, 1834, Van Buren Papers, LC.
50. *Senate Documents,* 23rd Congress, 1st Session, Vol. VI, document 459.
51. The most vigorous presentation of this thesis can be found in Bray Hammond, *Banks and Politics,* 326–450. It can also be found in more subdued tones in Nathan Miller, *The Enterprise of a Free People*

ing that the killing of the BUS was primarily the work of one man, and that man was Andrew Jackson. True, he had essential support from a great corps of friends, most of them named above, but the purpose, drive, and urgency to exterminate the monster emanated from Jackson.

The pity is that the War could have been avoided, that the Bank need not have been tormented and slain. Had Biddle not challenged Jackson's pride and position as President and leader of the Democratic party, it is very probable a compromise could have been hammered out extending the life of the charter. But once the Bank was attacked by the President, Biddle and his advisers demanded a showdown, and Jackson felt obliged to respond with total warfare. He slammed into the Bank with all the fury he normally reserved for Indians, British invaders, and cantankerous politicians.

Not that Jackson is guiltless. He came to the presidency burdened with some pretty weird ideas about paper money, along with an irrational prejudice against the BUS and a firm determination to change its character. In a sense, he courted trouble from the beginning. Still, he undoubtedly thought he could arrive at a sensible compromise with the Bank by which his worst objections could be eliminated. But it did not work out that way, and once the battle was joined, hope for compromise rapidly vanished.

Thus, in examining the Bank War, it is not so much a question of *who* killed this financial cock-of-the-walk—since the answer to that question is blindingly clear to anyone who studies the sources—but *why*. Why did Jackson do what he did? How did he convince the American people to accept his judgment to destroy the Bank? And what were the long-range effects of the War? These questions deserve brief attention in order to provide direction and focus before plunging into the involved history of the War itself.

The answer to the first question seems fairly certain. Initially, Jackson's financial losses during the Allison affair conditioned him against the Bank; his state rights views probably

(Ithaca, 1962), Irene Neu, *Erastus Corning* (Ithaca, 1960), and Lee Benson, *The Concept of Jacksonian Democracy* (Princeton, 1961).

caused him to challenge the Bank's constitutionality; and, certainly, the conventional Western prejudice played a part. But the one factor that converted prejudice into open hostility was political. Jackson seriously contended that the Bank was dangerous to the liberty of the American people because it concentrated enormous power in private hands and used this power to control legislation, influence elections, and even manipulate the operation of the government to get what it wanted. The Bank, said Jackson, was a monopoly with special privileges granted by the government; it exercised formidable sway over the affairs of the American people yet it was independent of presidential, congressional, or popular regulation. And because Jackson was a man who was exceedingly conscious of power, as well as jealous of his own presidential prerogatives, he was resentful of the Bank and conditioned even before he took office to demand changes in its operations.[52]

The political motive, then, is central to the Bank War. Other motives are unquestionably present but they do not begin to compare in importance to this single factor. Jackson's letters and conversations throbbed with anger over the Bank's "power to control the Government and change its character. . . ." He blasted the BUS as an "irresponsible" institution spending its money "as a means of operating upon public opinion." He dubbed it a "vast electioneering engine." [53]

A year or so after the Bank War had begun, Roger B. Taney, Jackson's Attorney General, summed up the administration's complaints against the corporation. He listed "its corrupting influence . . . its patronage greater than that of the Government—its power to embarrass the operations of the Government —& to influence elections. . . ." [54] These were all fundamentally political reasons, and the last-named—"to influence elections"— was the one that tormented Jackson, the one cited in almost every presidential paper, and the one his advisers harped upon whenever they wanted to activate the old man's temper.

52. Jackson to Lewis, April 29, 1833, Jackson-Lewis Papers, NYPL; Jackson to Overton, June 8, 1829, Jacob Dickinson Papers, TSL.
53. Richardson, *Messages and Papers of the Presidents,* II, 1224–1238.
54. Taney to Thomas Ellicott, January 25, 1832, Taney Papers, LC.

Specifically, the President heard stories that in state after state the BUS had employed its funds in 1828 to defeat his election and the election of other Democrats. Such interference in the electoral process, he rumbled, threatened "to destroy our republican institutions." Whether the charges were true or not can be, and were, debated; but Jackson believed them, and believed them so passionately that just three months after his inauguration he told John Overton, a friend of the BUS, that he planned to change "the present incorporated Bank to that of a National Bank—This being the only way that a recharter to the present U.S. Bank can be prevented & which I believe is the only thing that can prevent our liberties to be crushed by the Bank & its influence—for I [have learned] of the injurious effect of the directors of the Bank had in our late election which if not *curbed* must destroy the purity of the right of suffrage." [55]

"Curbed!" The Bank, or the "effect & interference" of its directors (Jackson sometimes switched meaning in the middle of a sentence), had to be curbed, not destroyed. The Bank, he decided, was excessively privileged and therefore dangerous and unconstitutional. So he would simply go to Washington and induce Congress to change the charter. Because he was only asking for alterations in the Bank's operations he did not expect a fight; but if one should develop he was certainly not the man to back away from it.

The second question posed above—how did Jackson convince the American people to go along with him in his condemnation of the Bank despite their own sympathies for the BUS—is more difficult to answer. It is difficult because of the strong probability that Jackson never did convince the electorate of the necessity of eliminating the BUS. He took the issue to them in the election of 1832, and although they reelected him to the presidency they did so in spite of his Bank stand. They reelected Jackson because they revered him, felt confidence in his administration of their affairs, and responded with affection to his obvious devotion to their interests. In addition, the Democratic party was extremely efficient in rounding up support for

55. Jackson to Overton, June 8, 1829, Jacob Dickinson Papers, TSL.

him. However, there is some evidence to suggest that Jackson's bank policy lost him more votes in the election than it gained him.[56] Many people and party leaders turned away from him because of his policy, and it was not until Biddle retaliated by curtailing loans and precipitating an economic panic in the winter of 1833-34 that the people came to recognize the merit of Jackson's complaints. In view of the considerable pro-Bank sympathy within the country and within Congress, it is remarkable that Jackson succeeded in destroying the BUS. If nothing else, it is a tribute to his consummate political skill in handling the electorate and the members of Congress.

Still, if Jackson was such an astute politician, and if he had any inkling of popular feeling about the Bank, why did he risk his reelection over the issue of recharter? Undoubtedly the reasons are varied; and to some extent he had little choice given Biddle's application for renewal in 1832. But perhaps the most important reason was Jackson's own wish to buttress presidential power with mass support—something never done before—and whether that support was given because of the issue itself or because of his enormous personal popularity was quite irrelevant. Once he had obtained mass approval he could then confront Congress with vastly strengthened institutional prerogatives, escalate the War if he chose, and, most important of all, force greater control over the direction of public affairs.

The changes Jackson inaugurated in the presidency introduces the final question involved in the War, namely the long-range effects of the destruction of the Bank upon the country and its institutions. Again, historians are sharply divided: some insist that Jackson's arrogance wrecked a splendid organization and initiated a century of unsound finance that made possible the chaotic business conditions of the Gilded Age;[57] others applaud the destruction of the Bank as a needed action against an overprivileged corporation that had the ability and sometimes the will to hobble business and bully the government.[58]

56. Remini, *Jackson,* 154–156. See also an analysis of the election in chapter IV of this book.
57. Govan, *Biddle, passim;* Hammond, *Banks and Politics, passim;* Van Deusen, *The Jacksonian Era,* 90.
58. Schlesinger, *Age of Jackson, passim;* Remini, *Jackson,* 167–168.

But whatever interpretation one adopts, the fact is undeniable that Jackson's War against the Bank profoundly enhanced the power of the presidency. Even if he was wrong in crushing the monster, when curbing it would have been sufficient, even if he launched the country upon a long period of economic instability—and these are by no means certain—it is indisputable that Jackson, by his actions, transformed and permanently strengthened the executive arm of the government.

Once Jackson marked the Bank for execution, he made good his intention, this despite tremendous opposition both within and without his party. What state legislatures, state courts, and sundry individuals had repeatedly attempted and failed to do, he accomplished. It was no mean feat to pull down the BUS. Because the Bank was a powerful agency, well entrenched in the country, it would not disappear just because the President wished it to. His accomplishment, therefore, was more than a personal victory, more than a tribute to his popularity, and more than a testament to his abilities as a politician. It was an acknowledgment of the enhancement of presidential power.

As Jackson implemented executive prerogatives in his pursuit of the Bank, some citizens became deeply alarmed. They denounced him as a dictator, labeled him "King Andrew I," and mourned the passing of constitutional government. Some even contended that he had weakened the presidency by his aggressiveness because he had set an impossible standard for his successors who would (and often did) shrink from using the powers he had acquired for the executive office. All the same, once the powers were exercised they were available, ready to be employed again by such future strong Presidents as Lincoln, the Roosevelts, Wilson, and Truman. In other words there was genuine institutional growth of the presidency under Jackson, not simply an expansion of power that contracted to its previous size after he left office.

The Bank War had another long-range effect. It reemphasized the Jacksonian concept that the President is the *only* elective officer of the national government representing *all* the people. Members of Congress represented states, fragments of states, or possibly sections and economic groups; but the President had a larger responsibility. His constituency cut across all sections and classes and economic divisions and encompassed the entire mass of the American people. Previous presidents, when they collided with Congress, usually had nowhere to turn because they lacked an immediate power base to fall back on for support. Consequently, they tended to act like prime ministers in their relations with Congress, much in the British tradition.

Jackson changed that. When he struck down the Bank charter he simply turned to the country and asked for popular support. This was the first time in American history that a major issue was taken directly to the electorate for decision. Although many people had grave doubts about the wisdom of crushing the Bank, they reaffirmed their faith in the President during the election of 1832. With this support as his power base, Jackson informed the members of Congress of his intention to destroy the Bank. Congressmen thundered their opposition, with the Senate finally censuring Jackson to prove its point. All to no avail. Jackson stormed after the BUS and did not pause until the monster was dead. In the course of this pursuit he redefined the character of his office and its relation to the American people. The presidency was never quite the same again.

2

The Confrontation

WHEN JACKSON entered the White House in March, 1829, he brought with him an unshakable resolve that something had to be done about the Bank of the United States. Maybe not much, but something. Occasionally he would let off steam before a group of close friends about the practices of the Bank, and once—prior to taking office in fact—he got himself so worked up that he turned to Colonel James A. Hamilton, the son of Alexander Hamilton, and with all the certitude of total ignorance, blurted out: *"Colonel, your Father was not in favor of the Bank of the United States."* The words knocked Hamilton speechless, and he just stared at Jackson in disbelief, not knowing what to say. It was one of those absurb remarks for which there was no appropriate answer.[1] Some time later, after he arrived in Washington as President-elect, Jackson considered using his inaugural address as the vehicle to notify the country of his concern about the Bank, but according to a tradition in Washington he was talked out of it by Martin Van Buren.[2]

Although the Bank was not a prominent issue in the presidential election of 1828, there were isolated reports that the BUS had spent its money to aid the cause of the National Republican party, which was the party of Henry Clay and the in-

1. James A. Hamilton, *Reminiscences of James A. Hamilton* (New York, 1869), 69.

2. Catterall, *Second Bank of the United States,* 184, n. 1, and Govan, *Biddle,* 115, n. 8 believe the tradition. Parton, *Jackson,* III, 258–259 doubts it, and I am inclined to agree with Parton. Van Buren's influence over Jackson was very slight at the beginning of the administration, so much so that he seriously considered resigning his post as Secretary of State. See Van Buren, *Autobiography,* 266.

cumbent President, John Quincy Adams. And these reports
were relayed to Jackson, usually by such men as Kendall who
harbored deep prejudices against the Bank. It was asserted, for
example, that money had been spent in Kentucky to persuade
roughnecks and river bums to vote for Adams; also, that the
branch bank in Louisville had donated $250 to the National
Republican party and that the money had financed the equip-
ment of "several grog-shops" to capture the votes of "boatmen
and loose characters." In Ohio, the Democratic party's leading organizer, T. P. Moore, informed Jackson that "Mr. Clay
presses the United States Branch Bank. . . ." Just what that
meant was not altogether clear, but it was enough to agitate
Jackson's already aroused suspicions.[3]

As more of these accusations came to his attention, Jackson
referred them to his advisers and asked that they be checked
out. Accordingly, in January 1829, Senator Richard M. Johnson of Kentucky wrote John McLean, the postmaster general,
who had supported Jackson in the recent election and would
soon be appointed to the Supreme Court by the new President,
and asked him to speak to Biddle. Specifically Johnson wanted
Biddle to investigate charges that the directors of the Louisville
and Lexington branches had actively advanced the candidacy
of Adams and had deliberately refused loans to members of
the Democratic party. McLean immediately complied. "The
members of Congress from Kentucky favourable to the new
Administration," he wrote Biddle, "are under the impression
that during the late elections in that State, great facilities, by
the state branches, were given to those persons, who were favourable to the reelection of Mr. Adams, whilst almost all
accomodations was withheld from the other side of the contest." Then McLean shot in a sly hint. Directors for the Kentucky branches should be selected from both parties, he
advised. "Being friendly to the Bank myself, I should regret to
see a political crusade got up against it. Some, I know are
ready to engage in this course. . . ."[4]

3. T. P. Moore to Jackson, June 13, 1827, Jackson Papers, LC; statement dated December, 1830, Jackson Papers, LC.
4. McLean to Biddle, January 5, 1829, Biddle Papers, LC.

It was a clear warning. Unfortunately, Biddle did not recognize how portentous it was. Compulsively defensive whenever his Bank was attacked, he replied to McLean that he had "never heard of any suspicion even, that any officer of the Bank has intermeddled with politics, except on one occasion, and that suspicion, I am satisfied after inquiry, was without foundation." [5] Biddle frankly did not believe any of the critical reports he had received about the Kentucky banks and said so to the cashier of the Lexington branch; however, since the request for an investigation had come from such a high source he agreed to look into the matter. But instead of conducting an impartial investigation, he asked a committee of the men from the very local branches under attack to submit a report, and not unexpectedly their report exonerated the branch banks from all impropriety. As for McLean's suggestion about appointing directors to the Kentucky branches from the Democratic party, a suggestion reiterated by Jacksonian Congressmen, it was impossible to do so, they said, since the gentlemen proposed by that party were "unfit." [6]

Biddle's failure to give satisfaction to a genuine grievance repeatedly cited in Kentucky was his first mistake. In fairness it should be stated that he was extremely anxious to keep the Bank out of politics.[7] Only his branch officers were not as circumspect as he, and when they were accused of political favoritism Biddle defended them despite contrary evidence.

A little later, Biddle compounded his first mistake by his negative response to a second complaint. This time the charges of mismanagement and political interference came from New Hampshire, and like the Kentucky accusations they were initiated by a number of influential Jackson men. Senator Levi Woodbury, an important figure in the organization of the Democratic party in New Hampshire and a future Secretary of the Treasury, complained to Biddle about Jeremiah Mason, the

5. Biddle to McLean, January 11, 1829, Biddle Papers, LC.

6. Biddle to John Harper, January 9, 1829, E. Shippen to Biddle, January 24, 1829, Biddle Papers, LC.

7. Biddle to Nicholas Devereaux, February 17, 1831, Biddle to C. C. Cambreleng, May 14, 1829, Biddle to Webster, February 16, 1826, Biddle to John Harper, January 9, 1828, Biddle Papers, LC.

president of the Portsmouth branch of the BUS, and, as expected, recited the familiar charges: the branch had been discriminatory in awarding loans; it refused the applications of the friends of General Jackson; it adversely interfered in the election of Democrats; and its operations were detrimental to the stockholders and to the community as a whole.[8]

It was common knowledge that for years the Portsmouth branch had been mismanaged. Indeed, one of the reasons for Mason's recent appointment was to initiate needed reforms. As it turned out, however, Mason was a close friend of Daniel Webster, the Senator from Massachusetts, who had campaigned vigorously against Jackson in 1828, and the friends of the General now regarded Mason's appointment as "odious," particularly since his management seemed to them "partial" to the National Republicans. Admittedly, it was a sticky situation, but as in the Kentucky furor, Biddle tended to discredit the criticisms he received against Mason and then dismiss them. "Such complaints," he told Robert Lenox, "are generally ill founded, & we are disposed to receive them with great distrust."[9]

When Woodbury informed Biddle of the party's complaints, he also wrote to Jackson's new Secretary of the Treasury, Samuel D. Ingham of Pennsylvania, a close friend of the Vice President, John C. Calhoun. Ingham was important enough, but Calhoun had played a significant role in the passage of the Bank charter in 1816 and his good will, as far as Biddle was concerned, was worth cultivating. Thus, when Ingham subsequently wrote Biddle, transmitting Woodbury's grievances, his letter merited respectful handling. But what added a note of urgency was Ingham's remark that he had received similar complaints about the Louisiana and Kentucky branches and that these would be sent to Biddle directly.

At this juncture, a cunning political operator entered the dispute. Isaac Hill emerged from the background and admitted instigating the charges against Mason in the first place. He was a short, lame, and cadaverous-looking man, formerly

8. Woodbury to Biddle, June 27, 1829, Woodbury Papers, LC.
9. Biddle to Lenox, July 6, 1829, Biddle Papers, LC.

editor of the New Hampshire *Patriot,* now second Comp-
troller of the Currency, soon to be United States Senator from
New Hampshire and later acknowledged as a member of Jackson's Kitchen Cabinet. In revealing his part in the plot against
Mason, Hill wrote to Biddle and freely admitted his animus,
stating flatly that the "friends of General Jackson have had but
too much reason to complain of the branch bank at Portsmouth." They now ask, he said, "that this institution . . .
may not continue to be an engine of political oppression." [10]
Curtly, he faulted Mason for lending money to his brother-in-
law in Boston, but refusing to accommodate "our" merchants
"with two or three thousand dollars." [11]

Unless he was hopelessly obtuse, Biddle could not doubt that
his Bank was in serious trouble with several men close to the
President. Still he remained calm, for he knew that men even
closer to Jackson than Hill supported the Bank, longtime Tennessee cronies such as William B. Lewis, John Overton, and
George Washington Campbell. So, ignoring Hill's letter, Biddle
replied to Ingham in what can only be described as bad temper.
He categorically denied that the Bank had interfered in the
recent elections, attributed the "personal rancor" against Mason
to his vigor in enforcing the payment of debts, and concluded by
saying that he would never tolerate the Bank becoming the instrument of party politics, whether it was the politics of the
Democratic party or the National Republican party. Biddle's attitude shocked Ingham. Although he did not assume the charges
against the Portsmouth branch were true, Ingham did object "to
a course of action which either resists inquiry, or, what is of the
same tendency, *enters upon it with a full persuasion that it is not
called for.*" [12]

Wisely, Biddle now decided to travel to Portsmouth and
investigate the charges personally, but instead of going to discover the truth, he left Philadelphia with his mind already set
on exonerating Mason. For the sake of appearance, he visited

10. Hill to J. N. Barker and John Pemberton, July 17, 1829 in *House
Report,* 22nd Congress, 1st Session, 472.

11. *Ibid.*

12. Quoted in Parton, *Jackson,* III, 264.

the branch, executed the outward motions of an investigation, spent several days interviewing those who could offer evidence, and finally concluded that the whole thing was a "paltry intrigue got up by a combination of small bankrupts & smaller Demagogues—that if the choice were to be made again, we ought to choose Mr. Mason." [13] Sad! Perhaps Mason deserved his post and maybe it was a "paltry intrigue," but to label the accusers "small bankrupts & smaller Demagogues" called into question Biddle's judgment, prudence, and good sense.

Meanwhile the plot against the New Hampshire branch widened when the Secretary of War, John Eaton, notified Mason that the pension fund for Revolutionary War veterans, which was handled by the BUS through its branches, would no longer be processed in Portsmouth, and that the books, papers, and money belonging to the pension agency and under the supervision of the War Department were to be switched to Concord and surrendered to a new agent when he called for them. This was pettiness, but a clear indication that the Bank was dealing with people bigger than "small bankrupts." Mason, on receiving the order, asked for instructions from Philadelphia and was immediately directed to refuse the Secretary's request and to express doubt at Eaton's legal right to make the request in the first place.

Thus, within a few months after Jackson's inaugural, a full-blown "conspiracy" appeared to be emerging against the Bank. Yet Biddle was not troubled. Worse, he aggravated the situation by his words and actions. Said he: "I will not give way an inch in what concerns the independence of the Bank, to please all the Administrations past, present or future." [14] Unfortunately he really believed he was being asked to investigate the branch banks "to please" the administration, rather than answer serious charges that the Bank in at least three or four states actively opposed Jackson's election and discriminated against Democrats in granting loans. And these requests had come from Cabinet members and other high officials. Hence, Biddle's insensitivity to the dangerous prejudices against the BUS,

13. Biddle to Cadwalader, August 28, 1829, Biddle Papers, LC.
14. Biddle to A. Dickins, September 16, 1829, Biddle Papers, LC.

along with his arrogance in refusing to deal appropriately with the requests of the Secretaries of Treasury and War, encouraged greater hostility toward his corporation.

After reviewing to his own satisfaction all the charges against Mason, Biddle informed Ingham on September 15, 1829, that the accusations were "entirely groundless." Furthermore, as a gesture of their confidence in Mason, the board of directors had reelected Mason to his post. Biddle gratuitously added that the board "acknowledge not the slightest responsibility of any description whatsoever to the Secretary of the Treasury touching the political opinions and conduct of their officers . . ." [15] It was a foolish and intemperate letter, one better written but never sent. In his need to assert his independence Biddle seemed willing to provoke a quarrel with the administration. To tell someone like Andrew Jackson what he could or could not do with respect to any agency created by the federal government clearly invited trouble.

Ingham handed Biddle's letter to the President. He offered no comment. Jackson read the document slowly and carefully. After a long pause, he quietly instructed the Treasury Secretary to inform Biddle that the President "reserves his constitutional powers to be exercised through Congress, to redress all grievances complained of by the people of the interference by the Branches with the local elections of the states, and all their interference with party politicks, in every section of our country, where those complaints have reach the Executive." [16]

In the minds of many contemporaries the Portsmouth incident was the initial explosion that triggered the Bank War. And Isaac Hill was credited with igniting the fuse. Opposition newspapers frequently advanced this claim, contending that Hill's failure "to revolutionize the Portsmouth Branch" set in train the events that ended with the annihilation of the Bank.[17] Thirty years later this theory was still current. James Parton, in researching his biography of Andrew Jackson in the late

15. Biddle to Ingham, September 15, 1829, *House Reports,* 22nd Congress, 1st Session, 456.

16. Jackson's Memorandum on Biddle's letter, 1829, Jackson, *Correspondence,* IV, 85.

17. *National Intelligencer,* September 11, 1832.

1850's, heard the allegation and found sufficient evidence to be convinced himself. "I believe myself warranted in the positive assertion," he wrote, "that this correspondence relating to the desired removal of Jeremiah Mason was the direct and real cause of the destruction of the bank. If the bank had been complaisant enough to remove a faithful servant, General Jackson, I am convinced, would never have opposed the rechartering of the institution." [18]

Considering the sources available to Parton when he wrote his book this was a good stab at a valid interpretation. Still, it was wrong. The Portsmouth incident was an important bit of evidence marshalled against the Bank, but it did not start the War. Quite apart from Hill's intrigue, and earlier than many realized, Jackson planned to force the Bank to accept changes in its operations.[19] So whether Mason remained or retired was incidental to Jackson's purposes; the President meant to "curb" the Bank and rid it of its "unconstitutional" features; his intentions were quite independent of what went on in New Hampshire.

But why did he wait so long before announcing his intentions? It was now six months since his inauguration and all he had done was listen to rumors and ask for investigations. In part his delay was caused by a sense of caution which warned him to go slowly, particularly in taking on so powerful an institution as the BUS. He also needed more time to build his case against the Bank and win allies beyond those he already had. But most of all he was distracted by other problems, most notably the scandal that wracked his administration over the marriage of his Secretary of War, John Eaton, to the notorious Peggy O'Neale.

Margaret O'Neale was the daughter of a Washington innkeeper and the widow of John Timberlake, a purser of the U.S. Navy. Because of an unsavory reputation she was socially ostracised after her marriage to Eaton. The wives of the other Cabinet officers, led by Mrs. Floride Calhoun, wife of the Vice President, refused to call on her or attend functions in which she was a

18. Parton, *Jackson*, III, 260.
19. Hamilton, *Reminiscences*, 69.

guest. Jackson was furious over their conduct, tending to see in Peggy something of his dead wife, Rachel, whose life was scarred by similar mistreatment. So, as the scandal deepened, Jackson did not press Biddle for an explanation of the Bank's interference in politics, even when he heard additional complaints against the branch bank in New Orleans.

By October 1829, Biddle was edgy about the way things were going. In an effort to make peace without granting concessions, he wrote to William B. Lewis, Jackson's long-time adviser and a friend of the BUS, asking him to show the President an enclosed letter from one Walter Dun, a member of the Lexington branch bank board. Dun's letter vehemently denied that the Lexington branch had ever played political favorites or was guilty of the other charges rumored against it. After showing the letter to Jackson, Lewis replied to Biddle that the President frankly admitted his suspicions about the Lexington branch but that he was pleased to "learn that probably there was no just cause for those complaints. . . ." Lewis continued. "He requests me to say, that he has too much confidence in you to believe, for a moment, that you should knowingly tolerate such conduct in the Branches of your Bank. . . ." After that obvious and needless bit of flattery which Lewis had been instructed to pass on, Jackson flashed his knife. He told Lewis to repeat in his letter to Biddle the complaints heard against the New Orleans branch and state that "an inquiry into the cause of those complaints and a removal of the ground if there be any for them, is an object, he thinks, worthy of the attention of the Parent Bank." [20]

Again an investigation. And, again, a demand for the removal of the cause. Biddle quickly replied to Lewis that the President would have satisfaction sooner than expected. It just so happened that Samuel Jaudon, the cashier of the New Orleans branch and a son-in-law of Senator Hugh Lawson White of Tennessee, was visiting Philadelphia and upon the receipt of Lewis' letter Biddle had ordered Jaudon to depart for Washington posthaste "to satisfy the President . . . that the state-

20. Lewis to Biddle, October 16, 1829, Biddle Papers, LC.

ments he had heard, are erroneous. . . ." [21] Jaudon shot
down to the capital as fast as arrangements could be concluded
and was received by Jackson the day he arrived. Acting the
soul of candor, the President confessed collecting documentation claiming there had been "a perversion of [the branch's]
influence to party purposes" but was gratified to hear Jaudon's
denials and to know that "no hostility to his administration was
exercised by the Board of the Parent Bank. . . ." [22]

It is possible Jackson was placated by Jaudon's denials, but
not likely. In several interviews with Bank personnel at this
time, he seemed slightly devious and disingenuous, pretending
he was openminded while all the time convinced of the Bank's
iniquity.[23] Meanwhile, Biddle was so anxious to learn whether
Jackson was satisfied with Jaudon's evidence that he went
personally to see the President and obtain assurances that the
New Orleans matter had been put to rest. During their long
conversation the wily old politician played cat and mouse with
his guest. Nothing was said about the New Orleans or Lexington branches, which must have unnerved Biddle who came prepared to recite the old denials once more. Instead, Jackson was
graciousness itself. He gushed his thanks to the Bank president
for offering to pay the national debt by January 8, 1833, the
anniversary of the Battle of New Orleans. This noble object
was something the General devoutly desired, having declared
it a principal goal of his administration as early as his inaugural
address. As Biddle relaxed to the pleasant strains of these expressions of gratitude, the President's mood suddenly changed.
"I think it right to be perfectly frank with you," Jackson declared
in measured tones. "I do not think that the power of Congress
extends to charter a Bank out of the ten mile square [*viz.* the
District of Columbia]. . . . I have read the opinion of John
Marshall . . . and could not agree with him. . . . I feel very
sensibly the services rendered by the Bank at the last payment of the national debt & shall take an opportunity of de-
clarring it publicly in my message to Congress. That is my own

    21. Biddle to Lewis, October 21, 1829, Biddle Papers, LC.
    22. Jaudon to Biddle, October 26, 1829, Biddle Papers, LC.
    23. *Ibid.*, Biddle's Memorandum of a Conversation with A. Jackson,
n. d., Biddle Papers, LC.

feeling to the Bank—and Mr Ingham's also."

Before Biddle could respond to this announcement, the President reassumed a gracious aid. He twitted his guest for getting into difficulty with Ingham "thro' the foolishness" of Isaac Hill. He pretended the Portsmouth incident was nothing but an embarrassment to him. "Oh, that has all passed now," replied the obliging Biddle. At that, Jackson reared up and attacked the Louisville branch of the Bank for improper conduct, ending his accusations by promising to present the particulars to Biddle as quickly as they could be gathered.

When the Bank president took his leave, shaken somewhat but still optimistic, he expressed his gratitude "at this frank explanation. We shall all be proud of any kind mention in the message," he continued, "for we should feel like soldiers after an action commended by their General."

"Sir," replied the sly Jackson, "it would be only an act of justice to mention it." [24]

Of course the President had no intention of commending the Bank in his annual message to Congress. Quite the opposite. Not only did he intend raising serious questions about the present Bank but he was already involved in plans to propose a substitute banking system to Congress when it convened.[25] Several months earlier, Jackson had asked Felix Grundy, the beetle-browed, rough-and-tumble politician from Tennessee, to give him his best thoughts about how a new bank might be fashioned which would eliminate the frequently expressed constitutional objections. Grundy submitted a plan on October 22 that called for the establishment of a principal bank in Philadelphia with branches in all the states. In addition, the directors of the parent bank would be elected by Congress and the directors of each branch by their Congressional delegations. The bank's capital would be established at $40 million, and the profits of each branch would be used for internal improvements within their respective states.[26]

24. Biddle's Memorandum, Biddle Papers, LC.

25. Kendall to Blair, November 22, 1829, Blair-Lee Papers, PUL.

26. Grundy to Jackson, October 22, 1829, Jackson, *Correspondence,* IV, 83.

Grundy's scheme did not arouse Jackson's enthusiasm, however. Although he toyed with several different plans at this time, the President could not make up his mind about any one of them, acting as though he knew he had to support some form of national banking and yet could not bring himself to do it. So he vacillated. He considered one scheme, then another, and then a third, always ending where he started, not certain whether he wanted a central bank or just a government depository. Throughout the Bank War this uncertainty was repeatedly evidenced both in his letters and conversations, and it is extremely difficult at times to determine what he meant when he used the phrase "national bank"—whether a central bank, or a multi-branched federally chartered banking operation, or simply a bank located in the District of Columbia to act as a fiscal agent of the government. Most probably he was willing to experiment with any scheme that political necessity dictated. The only alternative he totally eliminated—and that decision did not come until 1832—was a continuation of Biddle's Bank. And even that decision he reached slowly and hesitantly.

His indecision can be seen in the variety of schemes he considered in 1829. At one point he suggested the idea of tying the BUS to the Treasury and restricting its note-issuing powers; at another, of creating a bank for deposit to serve as a government agent in the transfer of public funds; and at another, of providing a system somewhat resembling Grundy's proposal.[27] Amos Kendall informed Blair that Jackson "has a scheme of a Bank purely national with branches in each state whose directors shall be chosen by the state Legislature subject to the control of the principal bank and removable by the President, the whole capital to be furnished by the U.S. and all its managers to have salaries. How would this do?" asked Kendall. *"Think* of this and give me your views, but do not *speak* of it as coming from this quarter." [28]

By the late fall of 1829 Jackson had definitely decided to

27. Jackson to Hamilton, December 19, 1829, Hamilton, *Reminiscences,* 151–152; Ingham to Jackson, November 26, 27, 1929, Berrien to Jackson, November 27, 1829, Jackson, *Correspondence,* IV, 92–95.
28. Kendall to Blair, November 22, 1829, Blair-Lee Papers, PUL.

lay the whole Bank business before Congress when it convened in December. But what was dangerous and foolhardy about all this was his readiness to tinker with the credit and currency structure of the country without preparing something else to substitute in its place. This mania to plunge ahead without knowing precisely where he was going alarmed several members of the Cabinet, including Martin Van Buren, the Secretary of State and heir-hopeful of the presidency. Van Buren, known as the Little Magician in recognition of his political skill, had advanced his standing recently as Jackson's successor because of the President's protracted quarrel with John C. Calhoun over the Eaton affair.[29] Van Buren was therefore wary of the Bank business lest it stunt his presidential chances.

Since the President had an extremely high regard for Colonel James A. Hamilton, his ad interim Secretary of State before Van Buren assumed the office, both Van Buren and William B. Lewis decided to ask Hamilton to speak to Jackson about his forthcoming message to Congress, particularly that section dealing with the Bank. Delighted to oblige, Hamilton accepted the invitation and arrived in Washington on November 27. He went directly to Van Buren's house and after dinner was taken to see Jackson.

There was a short conversation between Hamilton and the President, at the end of which the Colonel was invited to come back the next day for breakfast. When he returned, he was shown a draft of the annual message which Jackson had been preparing for the past several weeks with the aid of several assistants. Thumbing quickly through the manuscript to find what he was looking for, Hamilton discovered that the Bank had been "attacked at great length in a loose, newspaper, slashing style," which probably means that Amos Kendall authored the passage. Hamilton was then asked to lend a hand in editing and revising the message. This he readily agreed to do. Beginning immediately, he worked on the docu-

29. At the beginning of Jackson's administration it seemed certain that Calhoun was next in line for the presidency, but after the scandal to discredit Eaton through his wife, which Mrs. Calhoun abetted, and later with Calhoun's advocacy of the doctrine of nullification, Van Buren raced ahead as the leading candidate to succeed Jackson.

ment straight through the night, ending at 4:00 A.M. the next morning.[30]

During the night, Jackson, who slept in the adjoining room, heard Hamilton moving around and stoking the fire. The President came in to investigate and seemed surprised to find Hamilton still dressed. "My dear Colonel," he said, "why are you up so late?" "I am at my work," replied Hamilton, "which I mean to finish before I sleep." Concerned, the President summoned his servant, who slept on a rug in his room, and instructed him to stay in the Colonel's room and keep the fire going. An hour later, Hamilton finally retired for the night.

At eight the next morning the Colonel informed the President his work was done. "What have you said about the Bank," came the quick response.

"Very little," was the reply.

There was an annoyed look on Jackson's face. Seeing it, Hamilton picked up his sheets and began to read what he had written. "The charter of the Bank of the United States expires in 1836," he said, "and its stockholders will most probably apply for a renewal of their privileges. In order to avoid the evils resulting from precipitancy in a measure involving such important principles, such deep pecuniary interests, I feel I cannot do justice to the parties interested too soon, to present it to the deliberate consideration of the legislature and the people. Both the constitutionality and the expediency of the law creating the bank are well questioned by a large portion of our fellow-citizens; and it must be admitted by all that it has failed in the great end of establishing a uniform and sound currency."

At this point, Hamilton stopped reading, indicating he had reached the end. Jackson looked up at him and said, "Do you think that is all I ought to say?"

"I think you ought to say nothing at present about the bank," retorted Hamilton in a tone severer than he intended.

Jackson laughed. "Oh! My friend, I am pledged against the bank, but if you think that is enough, so let it be."

When Hamilton finally left the White House he went straight to Van Buren. As he stepped into the room the Secre-

30. Hamilton, *Reminiscences,* 149–150.

tary immediately quizzed him. "Well, Hamilton what is done?"

"The work is done," the Colonel replied. "I could not induce him to let me omit everything as to the bank, and here is what he agrees to." Hamilton then read the short paragraph which Jackson had heard not many hours before. When he finished, the Colonel turned to the Secretary and exclaimed, "Van Buren, you are against the bank on the ground of its unconstitutionality."

"Oh! no," replied the wily Van Buren, "I believe with Mr. Madison that the contemporaneous recognition of the constitutional power to establish a bank by all the departments of the government, and with the concurrence of the people, has settled that question in favor of the power." [31] Considering who Hamilton was, that may have been just a typical Van Buren response, gracious as well as verbally overblown; but more than likely he really believed what he said.

So the decision was made. Jackson would confront the Bank with the charge of failing to provide a sound currency—which was really pretty ridiculous under the circumstances—and at the same time, resurrect the old constitutional question as though it had never been settled by Justice Marshall in the McCulloch case. Although many in his Cabinet opposed the decision, the President honestly believed he was acting in the public interest and that he had no choice but to do his constitutional duty and bring the matter before Congress. "The confidence reposed by my country," he wrote, "dictated to my conscience that now was the proper time, and, although I disliked to act contrary to the opinion of so great a majority of my cabinet, I could not shrink from a duty so imperious to the safety and purity of our free institutions as I considered this to be." [32]

No sooner was the decision settled than word of it leaked to the press. Kendall was the leak. Late in November, he wrote to Mordecai M. Noah, surveyor of the New York port and editorial associate of James Watson Webb and James Gordon Bennett for the New York *Courier and Enquirer,* and told him what the President planned. The next day, portions of Kendall's

31. *Ibid.,* 150.
32. Jackson to Hamilton, December 19, 1829, *ibid.,* 151.

letter, "with a head and tail" stuck to it, were published as an editorial in the *Courier*. It was the first "quasi-official" blast at the Bank to appear in any newspaper.[33]

Meanwhile Jackson prepared the final version of his message for the opening of Congress on December 7. When the old man worked on something this important he frequently scribbled short notes with his steel pen on any stray scrap of paper he could find and then tucked it into his enormous white hat for safe keeping. When he was ready to put it all together he dumped the contents of his hat into the lap of his secretary and nephew, Major Andrew Jackson Donelson, and told him to shape it into correct English.[34]

As the finishing touches went into the message, the President worked silently to bring about the reelection of Andrew Stevenson of Virginia as Speaker of the House of Representatives. This was essential for Jackson's developing plans, for any changes in the Bank would be shaped in the House and it was therefore necessary to elect a Speaker he could trust and maneuver. With each session of the Congress the President became more adept at political jockeying, continually intruding his presence inside the legislative branch and finally dictating membership of important congressional committees.

Not surprisingly, Stevenson was reelected to his post by the overwhelming vote of 152 out of 191 votes cast. The next day the President's message was sent down and read. On and on, the clerk droned out the words to the Congress, first about foreign relations, then electoral reform, rotation of offices, the debt, Indians, and the tariff. Not until the very end did the section about the Bank appear. Hamilton's paragraph was repeated, with some slight changes, followed by a closing sentence which said: "Under these circumstances, if such an institution is deemed essential to the fiscal operations of the Government, I submit to the wisdom of the Legislature whether a national one, founded upon the credit of the Government and its revenues, might not be devised which would avoid all constitutional difficulties and at the same time secure all the advan-

33. Parton, *Jackson*, III, 268–269.
34. *Ibid.*, 269.

tages to the Government and country that were expected to result from the present bank." [35]

There was now no question about Jackson's position. It was open and public. He placed the Bank on notice that he did not like the way things were presently constituted and that he wanted changes, though he did not indicate precisely what changes he had in mind. Immediately, through the mail and in the press, he got popular reaction, both pro and con. The con Jackson dismissed as the expected reaction of "all the sordid and interested who prise self-interest more than the perpetuity of our liberty, and the blessings of a free republican government." But the pro tickled him, not only because the expressions were "very flattering" in their praise of his position but because they came from all parts of the country: Virginia, New York, Ohio, North Carolina, and—surprisingly—Pennsylvania. Of course, reaction depended on interest and viewpoint. As Congressman Ebenezar Sage from New York put it, "I have twice read Andrew's message & think it a very good one, for the best of all reasons, because in all important points his Dox agrees with my Dox, which you know is the only way of determining what is orthodox & what hetrodox—I shall vote against rechartering the great bank. It is capable of raising too high a pressure for the safety of those who may come within the sphere of its action." [36]

It goes without saying that Biddle's "Dox" came no where near Andrew's "Dox." He regarded the message as the President's own—"not dictated nor suggested by any body else"—in which "honest tho' erroneous notions" were expressed about the Bank. Still he remained calm and said he did "not feel the least anxiety about this sortie." What he did regret was the loss of individual property it would occasion and the "wound" it would inflict on the credit of the country. As for the charter itself, scheduled to expire in 1836, Biddle denied any intention of asking for renewal at this time. "We have never had any idea of applying to Congress for a renewal of the Charter at the

35. Richardson, *Messages and Papers*, II, 1025.
36. Sage to John W. Taylor, December 28, 1829, Taylor Papers, NYHS.

present session," he wrote, "and of course should abstain from doing so now. Our whole system of conduct is one of abstinence and self defence." [37]

And whistling in the dark! Biddle told several people he met that he was convinced by the message that the President was essentially friendly toward the Bank. There was nothing to worry about, he contended, nothing at all.[38]

For his part, now that he had publicly aired his spite against the Bank, Jackson was content. "I have brought it before the people," he said, "and I have confidence that they will do their duty." [39] This willingness to bring an issue directly before the American electorate not only defines Jackson's concept of his role as President but indicates something about the nature of Jacksonian Democracy. The General believed in closing the gap separating the people from their government by summoning them to support whatever he wished to do. They responded, too. Not simply because he was a popular war hero whom they loved but because the quality of leadership which they so desperately desired in their chief executive was becoming more brilliantly visible in the presidency of Andrew Jackson.

37. Biddle to Alexander Hamilton, December 12, 1829, Biddle to Nathaniel Silsbee, December 17, 1829, Biddle Papers, LC.
38. Duff Green to James A. Hamilton, December 16, 1829, Jackson Papers, LC. Green said that no sooner did Biddle circulate this falsehood than "a consequent rise of six per cent on the price of stock ensued! ! Would it not seem that this was done for fraudulent purposes?"
39. Jackson to Hamilton, December 19, 1829, Hamilton, *Reminiscences,* 151.

3

The War Begins

~~~~~~

AS JACKSON began his long campaign to win popular support for his project of "curbing" the Bank of the United States, the Congress proceeded to tell him that his message, as far as it related to the Bank, was just so much political poppycock. The House Ways and Means Committee, chaired by George McDuffie of South Carolina, one of Calhoun's henchmen, took up the two points specifically raised by the President and returned a report in the spring of 1830 contradicting both of them. The report not only affirmed the constitutionality of the Bank, but insisted the Bank had provided a currency even more uniform than specie.[1] The Senate Finance Committee, chaired by General Samuel Smith of Maryland, brought in a similar report which glowed with praise for the Bank.[2] Small wonder, since Biddle himself wrote the report and submitted it to the Committee through Smith.

Biddle reprinted these reports at Bank cost and distributed them extensively through the country, much to Jackson's distress. Also, as part of his program, Biddle initiated a correspondence with William Lewis, Edward Livingston, and other pro-Bank friends of the President, trying to insinuate himself into the Jackson circle, thereby persuading the General that the Bank was really no monster and deserved "his sanction . . . were the Charter renewed by both Houses of Congress."[3] But Biddle misjudged his man. The more he operated the more he

1. *House Report,* 21st Congress, 1st Session, No. 358.
2. *Senate Document,* 21st Congress, 1st Session, No. 104.
3. Biddle to Lewis, May 8, 1830, Biddle Papers, LC; Catterall, *Second Bank,* 201.

annoyed the Hero, probably because his campaign proved
effective. For one thing, the Committee reports of Congress
nettled Jackson; for another, their extensive distribution
alarmed him. Newspapers were repeating phrases from the reports, adding derogatory comments about his arguments
against the Bank.[4] What blackened the President's mood was
the lack of adequate support in the Democratic newspapers,
particularly the *United States Telegraph,* edited by Duff Green,
which was supposed to be the administration organ. "The truth
is," said Jackson, "that he [Green] has professed to me to be
heart and soul against the Bank, but his idol [John C. Cal-
houn] controles him as much as the shewman does his puppits,
and we must get another organ to announce the policy, and defend the administration; in his hands, it is more injured than
by all the opposition." [5]

The dissatisfaction over Green's failure to carry out the
Telegraph's function as party mouthpiece eventually led to
the establishment of the Washington *Globe.* Kendall's good
friend and former colleague on the Kentucky *Argus of Western America,* Francis P. Blair, who shared Kendall's loathing
for the BUS, was brought to the capital to do the job of editing.
Jackson soon grew to appreciate Blair's talents as a journalist.
The editorials were lively, slashing pieces, never giving Biddle
quarter, always after him, hitting hard—and frequently low
The *Globe* began publication on December 7, 1830, and the
speed with which it was acknowledged as the newspaper of
Andrew Jackson and the Democratic Party was a tribute to the
effectiveness of the party organization. The word was simply
given to Congressmen who passed it along to all the leading
men in their state. "We have here a new Paper called the
Globe," wrote one man, "edited by the late editor of the Frankfort Argus. He is a man of talent, a gentleman, sagacious, dis-
creet and powerful. He comes here by *invitation.* We are his
supporters. I wish you to be." [6]

4. For example, see the Washington *National Intelligencer* during
the spring of 1830.
5. Jackson to Lewis, June 26, 1830, Jackson-Lewis Papers, NYPL.
6. C. S. Smith to John A. Dix, December 14, 1830, Dix Papers, CUL.

Biddle, all the while, went on with his own campaign, hoping to convince the President that the Bank merited his support. Through Lewis and others he began to inquire what the General would do if Congress, this session, renewed the charter; but the more he inquired the more he received equivocal answers. Very probably, if Biddle had come forward at this time and offered substantial changes in the Bank's operations which would have eliminated the President's constitutional misgivings, Jackson would have approved recharter—not that the General ever said this clearly or even made up his mind precisely what changes he demanded. The president of the Nashville branch of the BUS recognized he could not get a straight answer from Jackson, although he seemed convinced that a bill to recharter would not be vetoed. Major Lewis concurred in this, flatly declaring that if Congress extended the life of the Bank, the President would "not object to it." [7]

But this optimistic view was not exactly borne out in Jackson's second message to Congress, delivered in December 1830. "Nothing has occurred to lessen in any degree the dangers which many of our citizens apprehend from that institution as at present organized," he wrote. What, then, could be done? As a possibility—but one not to be taken literally— Jackson suggested that the Bank become a branch of the Treasury, based on public and individual deposits, without power to make loans or purchase property, "which shall remit the funds of the Government"; if it was thought advisable, the officers of the Bank would be permitted to sell bills of exchange at a moderate price. Since it was not a corporate body and had no stockholders, debtors, or property, it would not be "obnoxious to the constitutional objections which are urged against the present bank. . . ." More important, since it would have "no means to operate on the hopes, fears, or interests of large masses of the community, it would be shorn of the influence which make that bank formidable." Jackson concluded by saying that these suggestions were not so much a recommendation as a way of "calling the attention of Congress to the possible

7. Lewis to Biddle, May 25, 1830, Biddle Papers, LC.; Catterall, *Second Bank,* 201, n. 3.

modifications of a system which can not continue to exist in its present form" without causing collisions with the government.[8]

The message, despite a slight tone of belligerency, clearly intimated the President's willingness to compromise on the Bank issue if "modifications" could be found and approved. Also, it is unlikely he would have insisted on the scheme outlined in his message. After all, Jackson was a politician, and politicians work within flexible guidelines.

But would Biddle compromise? Several men told him that "altho' the President is decidedly in favor of a Bank such as he recommended to Congress, yet if a bill were to pass both houses, renewing the charter of the Bank of the United States *with certain modifications,* the President would not withhold his approval." [9]

With certain modifications! Biddle was compulsively defensive about his Bank and could not bring himself to accept modifications, at least not the kind that made a difference to Jackson. Although he later proposed a few alterations which he could tolerate, they were so inconsequential as to antagonize the President and raise doubts about Biddle's willingness to settle the dispute at all.

So once again, Biddle shrugged off Jackson's complaints. "All this stir about monopolies," he told Albert Gallatin, "will blow off like the vapor from a Steam Boat as soon as the question gets fairly under way." [10] Untroubled, Biddle returned to his campaign of propaganda, publishing dozens of articles in

8. Richardson, *Messages and Papers,* II, 1091–1092. Not much later in a letter to Moses Dawson dated July 17, 1830, Jackson explained the kind of bank he preferred: "merely a *national Bank of deposit,* with power in time of war to Issue its bills bearing a moderate interest, and payable at the close of the war which being guaranteed by the national faith, Pledged, and based upon our revenue, would be sought after by the monied Capitalist, and do away, in time of war, the necessity of *loans.* This is all the kind of a bank that a republic should have." Jackson, *Correspondence,* IV, 161–162.

9. R. Smith to Biddle, December 13, 1830, Biddle Papers, LC.

10. Biddle to Albert Gallatin, November 30, 1830, Gallatin Papers, NYHS. Biddle did not believe Jackson would compromise, so his attitude is doubly strange. He was convinced that "the President aims at the destruction of the Bank." Biddle to Jonathan Roberts, January 15, 1831, Biddle Papers, LC.

newspapers which supported the Bank and attacked the position of those who defended the administration.[11] When he was warned not to pay newspaper editors for printing his propaganda because it tended to prove the President's point that the Bank spent its money to influence politics, Biddle demurred. "The whole influence of his [Jackson's] government," he wrote in reply, "& of the presses subservient to his government, is employed in endeavoring to break down the Bank. In this situation, the Bank can only find safety in such explanations of its proceedings as will satisfy the country that it has been unjustly assailed & that its operations are highly beneficial. But how is it to make these explanations, except thro' the press, the only channel of communication with the people? And if it employs that channel, why should it ask of printers to insert its explanations gratuitously? If a grocer wishes to apprize the public that he has a fresh supply of figs, the printer whom he employs for that purpose never thinks of giving his labor for nothing, but charges him for his trouble in inserting the advertisement. If the Bank in a like manner wishes a printer to insert information about its concerns, why should it not pay him for his trouble?" [12]

While this skirmishing in the newspapers progressed, an unexpected event occurred which seemed to presage Biddle's complete salvation. This was the breakup of Jackson's first Cabinet, the causes of which had been developing for months. First, there had been dissension over the refusal of the wives of the Cabinet members to socialize with Peggy Eaton, the wife of the War Secretary; then, there was the rivalry between Van Buren and Calhoun, each trying to jockey the other out of the succession line; finally, there was the disclosure that Calhoun had sought Jackson's censure of the invasion of Florida in 1818 when Calhoun was a member of James Monroe's Cabinet. Van Buren, in one of his more brilliant moments, suggested that he might end the bickering within the official family by submitting his resignation as Secretary of State; then the other members could be pressured into resigning, and once that was done, Jack-

11. Catterall, *Second Bank,* 205.
12. Biddle to J. Hunter, May 4, 1831, Biddle Papers, LC.

son could reorganize his Cabinet and bring in replacements un-
contaminated by Calhoun's influence.

Jackson refused to allow Van Buren to sacrifice himself
until it was decided that the Magician could be compensated by
appointment as Minister to Great Britain. That settled, Van
Buren submitted his resignation as Secretary of State in April
1831, and was soon followed by the other members of Jackson's official family.

With the selection of the new Cabinet, Biddle felt the ex-
hilaration of a man whose worst fears had suddenly and totally
vanished. For, to his utter amazement, most of the new personnel recruited by the President were men who favored a national bank or some variation of it. Included were Edward
Livingston of Louisiana, a staunch defender of the BUS, as
Secretary of State; Lewis Cass, as Secretary of War; Levi
Woodbury of New Hampshire, as Secretary of the Navy; Roger
B. Taney of Maryland, who, as Attorney General, would emerge
as Biddle's only real enemy in the Cabinet; and, last but best of
all—for he was a known friend of the Bank—Louis McLane
of Delaware, as Secretary of the Treasury.

Biddle enthused over Jackson's splendid new Cabinet. To
begin with, it meant the riddance of Van Buren, whose influence on Jackson was considered prejudicial to the Bank's
best interests. Van Buren represented New York, and rumor
had it that New York bankers daily muttered a death-wish for
the BUS. Everything considered, events had suddenly and mir-
aculously brightened for Biddle. "I consider it a fortunate
change for the Bank," he commented, "by the substitution
of an avowed friend Mr. Livingston, for a decided enemy in
Mr. Van Buren. The new Secretary of the Treasury is also a
known friend and generally speaking the occurrence I consider
fortunate." [13]

Not much later Biddle had a long, private conversation
with this "known friend." Jackson was privy to the conference,
and indeed encouraged it because he wanted Biddle to know
that things had not really altered, despite the new faces in the
Cabinet. If anything, the President was more hostile to any

13. *Ibid.*

move on the part of the Bank to seek recharter during the present session of Congress for the explicit reason that it was a year in which Jackson must seek reelection to the presidency and he wished to avoid further controversy at this time. During the conference McLane emphasized this point, and he repeatedly warned Biddle against any action that could be interpreted as interfering in the election. If the President were tested by an application for a renewal, said McLane, "he would be more disposed to reject it on that very account. The Prest is now perfectly confident of his election—the only question is the greater or the less majority, but he is sure of success & wishes to succeed by a greater vote than at the first election. If therefore while he is so confident of reelection this question is put to him as one affecting his reelection, he might on that account be disposed to put his veto on it." Apparently it was all very well for Jackson to stir up the people against the Bank, but let Biddle retaliate—or appear to—by raising the issue in an election year, and he would jeopardize his charter. In return for Biddle's forbearance, McLane said he would recommend to the President the renewal of the charter, and Jackson, to extricate himself gracefully from the affair and "save appearances," would tell the members of Congress that the entire matter now rested solely with them.[14]

Biddle came away from the conference buoyed by McLane's promise to recommend renewal. Conceivably, at this moment, the Bank War could have ended, for Jackson, in his third annual message, delivered on December 6, 1831, essentially carried out his part of the "bargain." Although "to save appearances" he insisted his general attitude toward the BUS had not changed, he informed Congress that he was willing to go along with their decision on recharter and leave the issue entirely to their discretion. "Entertaining the opinions heretofore expressed in relation to the Bank," he said, ". . . I deem it proper on this occasion . . . to leave it for the present to the investigation of an enlightened people and their representatives." Simultaneously, McLane was permitted to

14. Biddle's Memorandum, October 19, 1831, Biddle Papers, LC.

argue for charter renewal in his annual Treasury report to Congress.[15]

But Jackson's tepid statement was not good enough for Biddle. In effect he wanted the President to reverse himself completely on the Bank issue and come out for recharter. But this Jackson would never do; it was too abject a surrender. If Biddle expected more than Jackson delivered, if he was misled by McLane in their conversation, then, said the President, McLane spoke for himself, "and has not committed me." [16] Despite his willingness to retreat, Jackson still entertained "the opinions heretofore expressed" about the Bank. "Mr. McLane and myself understand each other and have not the slightest disagreement about the principles, which will be a *sine qua non* in my assent to a bill rechartering the Bank." [17]

The moment had now arrived for bringing the two antagonists together and resolving the dispute. Jackson, wishing to safeguard his reelection in 1832, was withdrawing his active opposition toward recharter. There was nothing underhanded about this, simply the obvious move of a smart politician. He was probably afraid—and rightly so—of losing Pennsylvania if he continued the Bank fight, and since he wanted a decisive popular victory and a massive electoral vote, Pennsylvania was essential to him. So he backed off. Biddle, in the interest of protecting his Bank, should now have indicated his readiness to cooperate, arranged with the President for alterations in the charter, and followed a time schedule for introducing the rechartering bill into Congress which Jackson would dictate. The final result might not accord in every particular with what Biddle wanted, but, after all, that was the essence of compromise. At least he would preserve the national bank, or a reasonable facsimile,[18] and once Jackson accepted the compromise recharter was assured.

15. Richardson, *Messages and Papers,* II, 1121.

16. Jackson to John Randolph, December 22, 1831, Jackson Papers, LC.

17. Jackson to James A. Hamilton, December 12, 1831, Hamilton, *Reminiscences,* 234.

18. It was the opinion of several Congressmen that Jackson would only insist on "slight modifications" of the charter. Indeed, there is some

Instead of this, Biddle committed an incredible blunder. Despite the repeated warnings of McLane and others not to bait Jackson in an election year and despite the President's obvious gesture toward compromise, Biddle dismissed it all and plunged ahead with a request to Congress for recharter in 1832, four years before the date of expiration. By this single, calculated, foolish act, Biddle wrecked all hope for a peaceful solution to the issue and forever doomed his institution. "By deferring its application to next Session," wrote Senator Willie P. Mangum of North Carolina, "I have no doubt with but slight modification (to save appearances) it would have met with Executive favor. —It is *now* more than doubtful whether it will. —And the whole may ultimately take the appearance of a trial of strength between Gen Jackson & the Bank—In that case the Bank will go down—For Gen J's popularity is of *a sort* not to slaken [*sic*] at present." [19]

Why, then, did Biddle permit this lunacy? Why did he opt for a "trial of strength?" In part, he was afraid Jackson could not control his advisers and that sooner or later they would force him to a showdown. "What I have already dreaded about this new cabinet," he wrote in December, 1831, "was that the kitchen would predominate over the parlor." [20] Furthermore, Biddle figured that if Jackson feared to risk reelection over the issue, then it must indeed be a very good time to bring it up. Since he must request recharter before Jackson's second term ended, Biddle felt he had a better chance of getting it if he asked before the election rather than afterward. Then, if Jackson refused the request and vetoed the recharter bill, Congressional candidates up for election would have to commit themselves on the issue one way or another, and Biddle believed there were enough Americans who favored the Bank to elect

---

evidence that he was quite prepared to accept another national bank even at the conclusion of the War. Mangum to William Gaston, January 19, 1832, Henry T. Shanks, ed., *The Papers of Willie Person Mangum* (Raleigh, N. C., 1950), I, 456; Jackson to Woodbury, July 3, 1834, Woodbury Papers, LC; Benjamin F. Butler to Thomas W. Olcott, January 27, February 1, March 20, 1834, Olcott Papers, CUL.

19. Mangum to Gaston, January 19, 1832, Shanks, ed., *Papers of Willie P. Mangum,* I, 456.

20. Quoted in Govan, *Biddle,* 170.

a sufficient number of Congressmen to override the veto. Many leaders of the National Republican party argued this way, including John Quincy Adams, Daniel Webster, and Henry Clay—especially Clay, who had just been nominated by his party to run for the presidency against Jackson and desperately needed an issue that could neutralize Old Hickory's popularity and give him a sporting chance to win. "The friends of the Bank," Clay told Biddle, "expect the application to be made. The course of the President, in the event of the passage of a bill, seems to be a matter of doubt and speculation." [21]

Biddle knew this was false. He had been told by several men,[22] and most importantly by McLane himself, that if he tested the President with a "trial of strength" he would be hit with a veto. Even so, Biddle decided to gamble, and with it he risked the life of his Bank.

Along with the gamble went a crude threat of political blackmail. "For myself," wrote Biddle at this time, "I do not care a straw for him [Jackson] or his rivals—I covet neither his man servant—nor even his maid servant, his ox nor any of his asses. Long may he live to enjoy all possible blessings, but if he means to wage war upon the Bank—if he pursues us till we turn & stand at bay, why then—he may perhaps awaken a spirit which has hitherto been checked & reined in—and which it is wisest not to force into offensive defence." [23]

Jackson, too, must share the blame for the senseless rush to battle. He had whipped into Washington at the beginning of his administration with a determination to alter the character of the national bank. Yet when Biddle pressed him about his intentions toward recharter, the President responded equivocally. Then, suddenly, Jackson backed away from the contest

21. Clay to Biddle, December 15, 1831, Biddle Papers, LC.

22. "If the friends of the Bank pressed it now," Biddle was told by a pro-Bank politician, "it would be construed by the friends of the President as an act of hostility on him—that the President was not a man to be forced into any measure & would be more likely to veto the bill before the election than afterward. . . ." N. D. Merth to Biddle, December 14, 1831, Biddle Papers, LC. That same sentiment is also expressed in Thomas Cadwalader to Biddle, December 21, 1831, Biddle Papers, LC.

23. Biddle to Charles J. Ingersoll, February 11, 1832, Biddle Papers, LC.

in order to protect his reelection. Could it be a doublecross? How was Biddle to know that the President would not renew the War once he had secured a second term?

The regrettable decision to request recharter before the election gave the Bank's implacable enemies, men like Kendall, Hill, and Blair, the final piece of evidence they needed to clinch their argument that the monster was indeed a political agency quite prepared to tamper with the electoral process to get what it wanted. It was the one argument that both convulsed the President and convinced him to veto recharter. Said Taney: "Now as I understand the application at the present time, it means in plain English this—the Bank says to the President, your next election is at hand—if you charter us, well— if not, beware of your power." [24]

The deliberate baiting of Jackson changed the whole temper of the War. His fighting instincts aroused, the President reacted in character and stormed forward to battle the Monster of Chestnut Street. When James Hamilton spoke to him about being forced to grant the recharter, Jackson almost turned scarlet. "I will prove to them that I never flinch," he roared; "that they were mistaken when they expect to act upon me by such considerations." [25]

The battle was formally joined when a memorial for a renewal of the charter was submitted to Congress on January 6, 1832. Normally, General Samuel Smith, chairman of the Senate Finance Committee and a friend of the BUS, would have submitted the memorial, but he was not considered aggressive enough to do the Bank justice, so Senator George M. Dallas, a Democrat from Pennsylvania, was chosen to perform the honors.[26] In the House, George McDuffie, chairman of the Ways and Means Committee, shepherded the rechartering bill to the floor.

To lead the anti-Bank forces in Congress, Jackson chose the redoubtable senator from Missouri, Thomas Hart Benton, a forceful debater as well as an astute floor manager. Benton

24. Taney to Ellicott, January 25, 1832, Taney Papers, LC.
25. Hamilton to a friend, March 14, 1832, Hamilton, *Reminiscences,* 243.
26. Catterall, *Second Bank,* 223.

was a powerful-looking man with black curly hair, side whis-
kers and a long nose that wandered crookedly down his face.
Jackson had had a gun fight with Benton and Benton's brother
in Tennessee back in 1813 which ended with the General taking a slug in the shoulder and Benton, in the scuffle, being
pitched backward down a hotel staircase. But that was all in
the past. Benton was now Jackson's staunch ally, and his views
of paper money and banking corresponded exactly with those
of the President.

After several consultations between members of Congress
and the White House, a carefully-mapped course of action for
the Jacksonians was adopted. In the words of Benton, they were
"to attack incessantly, assail at all points, display the evil of
the institution, rouse the people—and prepare them to sustain
the veto." [27] It was splendid strategy; smart politics, too; and
just the sort of approach to appeal to the President. In line
with their overall plans, Benton proposed that Augustine S.
Clayton, a Georgian who had written a pamphlet excoriating
the BUS, introduce a resolution in the House of Representatives
calling for an investigation of the Bank for misconduct and
alleged violations of the charter.[28] Since it was widely gossiped
that a number of Congressmen were in the pay of the Bank—
Daniel Webster, for one—an investigation would start things
off with a smash. And the pro-Bank forces dared not object for
fear of offending their "intelligent constituency" who would con-
clude that Congress was "little inclined to look into the alleged
abuses of that mammoth moneyed aristocracy." [29] Under the
circumstances, therefore, Clayton's motion easily passed when
introduced in the House and a committee was immediately
formed to proceed to Philadelphia to inspect the Bank's operation.[30]

Naturally, Speaker Stevenson chose a committee hostile to

27. Thomas Hart Benton, *Thirty Years' View* (New York, 1856),
I, 235.

28. *Ibid.*, 236.

29. William L. Marcy to Thomas W. Olcott, January 22, 1832, Olcott
Papers, CUL.

30. The committee consisted of its chairman, Clayton, and Richard
M. Johnson, Francis Thomas, Churchill C. Cambreleng, George McDuffie,
John Quincy Adams, and John Watmouth.

the Bank, as Jackson expected him to do. Not unexpectedly, the final report of the committee shimmered with distortions about the BUS. Also, quite naturally, Biddle hampered the investigation at every step of the way, though the final report would not have been different even if he had cooperated to the fullest. When the document was finally published, the Washington *Globe* and other Democratic newspapers chorused their praise for the committee's excellent work and used the distortions of the document to launch a massive attack against the Bank. Impartial newspapers had a different view of the report, however. *Niles Weekly Register* called it " the strangest mixture of *water-gruel* and *vinegar,* the most awkward and clumsy and exaggerated *ex-parte* production that we ever read: it seems to have been begotten in passion and brought forth in weakness—still born!" [31]

The lines of battle in Congress now clearly drawn, each side attempted to organize itself to win support around the country. The Democrats went after the Workingmen's associations in the cities and encouraged them to identify the Bank as the major source of their economic plight. "Get the Workies to be up and doing on the U.S.B. question," wrote one Congressman. "They are democrats in principle." [32] Along with the workingmen, farmers, merchants, and manufacturers were also wooed in the general rush to convert Jackson's friends into enemies of the Bank. And it hardly mattered whether or not these groups benefited economically from the destruction of the BUS. Economics was a secondary consideration—and for some no consideration at all. The principal object was to line up support behind Jackson, in any way possible, and to accept anyone who would join. Democrats were indifferent to the ultimate economic changes that might ensue from their campaign tactics. Their goal was immediate, and it was political.

Meanwhile, Biddle hurried down to Washington to conduct the battle on the scene, ordering petitions be sent to Congress-

31. *Niles Weekly Register,* May 12, 1832. At the beginning of the War Niles was impartial; he later went over to the side of the Bank.

32. Churchill C. Cambreleng to Jesse Hoyt, February 16, 1832, William L. MacKenzie, *The Life and Times of Martin Van Buren* (Boston, 1846), 231.

men from every state in the Union.[33] Most of the petitions read alike, demanding renewal of the charter and predicting catastrophe if its passage failed. Caught in the cross fire of this opening round in the War were pro-Bank Jacksonians, a singular group of Congressmen who regarded the BUS as essential to the country but dared not break with the President over the issue. Several of them, therefore, went to Biddle and begged him to defer the bill for rechartering until after the election, again warning him that a veto was inevitable. But Biddle refused to budge.[34] So these bedeviled Democrats switched their strategy by introducing delaying tactics in Congress to hold the bill up until the next session. However, the well-disciplined Bank men beat them off. "Our life," said Thomas Cadwalader, Biddle's second-in-command, "depends on this session, and getting the veto now, so that the nation may be roused before the autumnal elections." [35]

On June 11, 1832, despite the heroic efforts of Benton and the other Jacksonian leaders in Congress, the bill for recharter passed the Senate by a vote of 28 to 20, and almost a month later, on July 3, rode through the House by 107 to 85. The vote reflected solid support for the Bank in New England and the Middle Atlantic states, strong opposition in the South, and almost divided opinion in the Northwest and Southwest. Biddle was ecstatic. "I congratulate our friends most cordially upon this most satisfactory result. Now for the President. My belief is that the President will veto the bill though this is not generally known or believed." [36]

Debilitated by the hot, sticky July weather, Jackson resembled a "spectre" close to death when the Bank bill reached his desk.[37] But his will to kill the monster kept him going. For now he no longer talked about compromising with Biddle or curbing the Bank's power and nudging it within the orbit of government control. Now he talked only of destroying the Bank outright. Yet, with all this talk, Jackson was too astute a

33. Cambreleng to Hoyt, February 5, 1832, *ibid.,* 231.
34. Catterall, *Second Bank,* 234.
35. Cadwalader to Biddle, May 31, 1832, Biddle Papers, LC.
36. Biddle to Cadwalader, July 3, 1832, Biddle Papers, LC.
37. Van Buren, *Autobiography,* 625.

politician to miss the danger to his reelection and the election of other Democrats by vetoing the bill. Still, he believed with almost religious fervor that he was acting for the public good in striking down this extragovernmental "power in the State." He felt the people would understand this and sustain him in the coming battle. And it was essential that they sustain him, he felt, if he was to represent them before the Congress. "Providence has had a hand in bringing forward the subject at this time," he told Kendall, "to preserve the republic from its thraldome and corrupting influence." [38] Thus, certain of popular approval and convinced of the Bank's evil influence, Jackson wrote the veto, doing it in such manner as to "leave the Subject *open* for the decision of the people at their next Election." [39]

The actual writing of the message was the work of several men: Jackson himself, Taney, Amos Kendall, Andrew J. Donelson, and Levi Woodbury.[40] What resulted was not a typical veto that simply directed itself to the constitutional issue, but a message that for the first time invoked political, social and economic, as well as strictly legal, arguments. Previous presidents had used the veto a total of nine times, but only on three occasions had important legislation been involved. Jackson vetoed twelve times, more than all his predecessors combined, and he negated bills for reasons that had nothing to do with their constitutionality. What he did in effect was to make the veto power an important presidential instrument in controlling legislation. Hereafter the threat of a possible veto for *any* reason forced the Congress to consider carefully the President's wishes on *all* bills before legislating them. This essentially changed the relationship between the legislative and executive branches, and immeasurably strengthened the latter. It was one of Jackson's important contributions to the development of presidential power; indeed, said one historian, Jackson

38. Jackson to Kendall, July 23, 1832, Jackson-Kendall Papers, LC.
39. Samuel Smith to Jackson, June 17, 1832, Jackson, *Correspondence*, IV, 449.
40. Traditionally, Roger B. Taney has been credited with being the principal author of the veto. Lynn L. Marshall, "The Authorship of Jackson's Bank Veto Message, *Mississippi Valley Historical Review* (1963) L, 466–477 argues persuasively that the honor really belongs to Amos Kendall.

successfully claimed that the weight of the chief executive was the equivalent of two-thirds of both houses of Congress.[41]

The Bank veto of July 10 is the most important presidential veto in American history. It was a powerful and dramatic polemic, cleverly written to appeal to the great masses of people and to convince them of the truth of its arguments. The President claimed that the Bank enjoyed exclusive privileges that gave it a monopoly of foreign and domestic exchange. Worse, eight millions of its stock were held by foreigners. "By this act the American Republic proposes virtually to make them a present of some millions of dollars," said Jackson— and why should the few, particularly the foreign few, enjoy the special favor of the country? "If our Government," he continued, "must sell monopolies . . . it is but justice and good policy . . . to confine our favors to our own fellow citizens, and let each in his turn enjoy an opportunity to profit by our bounty." Over and over, like the intense nationalist he was, Jackson reiterated his concern over this foreign influence within the Bank.[42]

Then the President turned to the constitutional question involved in the recharter. He noted that the Supreme Court in *McCulloch* v. *Maryland* had judged the Bank constitutional. "To this conclusion I cannot assent," he declared. Elaborating, he announced that the Congress and the President as well as the Court "must each for itself be guided by its own opinion of the Constitution. It is as much the duty of the House of Representatives, of the Senate, and of the President to decide upon the constitutionality of any bill or resolution which may be presented to them for passage or approval as it is of the supreme judges when it may be brought before them for judicial decision. The opinion of the judges has no more authority over Congress than the opinion of Congress has over the judges, and on that point the President is independent of both. The authority of the Supreme Court must not, therefore, be permitted to control the Congress or the Executive when acting in their legislative capacities, but to have only such influence as the force of their

41. Leonard D. White, *The Jacksonians* (New York, 1954), 29,
42. Richardson, *Messages and Papers,* II, 1140–1141, 1142–1144.

reasoning may deserve." [43] Ever since the writing of this passage Jackson has been unfairly faulted for attempting to make himself co-equal with the courts in determining the constitutionality of Congressional legislation. What he actually said was that no member of the tripartite government can escape his responsibility to consider the constitutionality of all bills and to vote or act as his good judgment dictates. And, in the matter of the Bank now before him, Jackson did not agree with the Supreme Court. Since the Bank recharter was subject to legislative and executive action, he simply claimed the right to think and act as an independent member of the government.

However, it was at the tail end of the message that Jackson detonated his political bombshell. In a calculated effort to intensify class antagonisms, he said: "It is to be regretted that the rich and powerful too often bend the acts of government to their selfish purposes. Distinctions in society will always exist under every just government. Equality of talents, of education, or of wealth can not be produced by human institutions. In the full enjoyment of the gifts of Heaven and the fruits of superior industry, economy, and virtue, every man is equally entitled to protection by law; but when the laws undertake to add to these natural and just advantages artificial distinctions, to grant titles, gratuities, and exclusive privileges, to make the rich richer and the potent more powerful, the humble members of society—the farmer, mechanics, and laborers—who have neither the time nor the means of securing like favors to themselves, have a right to complain of the injustice of their Government. There are no necessary evils in government. Its evils exist only in its abuses. If it would confine itself to equal protection, and, as Heaven does its rains, shower its favors alike on the high and the low, the rich and the poor, it would be an unqualified blessing. In the act before me there seems to be a wide and unnecessary departure from these just principles." [44]

Thus closed this extraordinary message. Bank men were aghast at its tone and language, and many of its principles

43. *Ibid.,* 1144–1145.
44. *Ibid.,* 1153.

were later scored by historians and economists as "beneath contempt." [45] Nicholas Biddle regarded the entire message as the rabble rousing cry of a deranged demagogue preaching anarchy.[46] But Democrats hailed it as a "Second Declaration of Independence" and employed its phrases and ideas during the election to incite the masses against the "rich and powerful." [47]

The message was totally indifferent to the Bank's genuine services to the nation. Indeed, it denied these services existed. As an economic document, therefore, attempting to prove a case, it can be easily shredded for misstating facts and for faulty reasoning; but as a political document, throbbing with the sounds that stir men to action, it was propaganda of the highest order. And that really was what Jackson wanted: fighting propaganda with which to rouse the people, obtain their support, and win reelection. Responsible men, however, thought it would have the reverse effect. Said one: "It ought to prostrate any man or any argument under Heaven. Mr. Webster, I think, will scatter it to the four winds of Heaven." [48]

On July 11, 1832, Webster rose in the Senate chamber to "scatter" the presidential veto. Speaking slowly at first but picking up speed as he bore down on his subject, he dissected the message section by section. He was contemptuous of its constitutional argument, outraged by its disrespect toward the Supreme Court, and angered by its efforts to divest Congress of its legislative authority. "According to the doctrines put forth by the President," intoned Webster, "although Congress may have passed a law, and although the Supreme Court may have pronounced it constitutional, yet it is, nevertheless, no law at all, if he, in his good pleasure, sees fit to deny it effect; in other words, to repeal and annul it." Webster's voice betrayed the faintest trace of anger as he continued. "Sir, no President and no public man ever before advanced such doctrines in the face of the nation. There never before was a moment in which any

45. Catterall, *Second Bank,* 239.
46. Biddle to Clay, August 1, 1832, Biddle Papers, LC.
47. See the editorials in the Washington *Globe* for August and September, 1832.
48. John G. Watmouth to Biddle, July 10, 1832, Biddle Papers, LC.

President would have been tolerated in asserting such a claim to despotic power."

Jackson's bold assertion of his prerogatives was not confined to a simple statement of presidential preeminence over the other two branches of the government. He went further. The message, declared Webster, also "claims for the President, not the power of approval, but the primary power, the power of originating laws." Study the words carefully, he said. "The message pretty plainly intimates that the President should have been *first* consulted," that he should have had a hand in framing the bill. Which means, of course, that all future legislation can be endangered unless there is prior consultation with the President! "Mr. President," the Senator concluded, "we have arrived at a new epoch. We are entering on experiments with the government and the Constitution, hitherto untried, and of fearful and appalling aspect." [49]

Clay buttressed all of Webster's arguments about Jackson's governmental innovations in a lengthy speech to the Senate delivered the same day Jackson sent down his message. He was particularly forceful in condemning the President's perversion of the veto power. "The veto," he remarked, "is an extraordinary power . . . not expected by the [Constitutional] convention to be used in ordinary cases. It was designed for instances of precipitate legislation, in unguarded moments." It was to be employed rarely, if at all. Clay reviewed the history of the power, noting how infrequently previous presidents had used it, in fact, not once by Jackson's immediate predecessor, John Quincy Adams. "We now hear quite frequently, in the progress of measures through Congress," he said, "the statement that the President will veto them, urged as an objection to their passage!" What kind of threat is that, he asked? Through the instrument of the veto, the President may effectively intrude into the legislative process and force his will upon the Congress. Such action, Clay concluded, was "hardly reconcilable with the genius of representative government." [50]

49. Daniel Webster, *Works of Daniel Webster* (Boston, 1864), III, 434, 446, 438, 447.
50. Henry Clay, *The Works of Henry Clay,* Calvin Colton, ed., (New York and London, 1904), VII, 524.

The realization by the Bank men that Jackson was expanding presidential power by striking down legislation for reasons of policy rather than constitutional reasons, and threatening the veto in order to gain greater influence over the legislative process, forced the Democrats into a spirited defense of Jackson's actions. In the Senate, Thomas Hart Benton assumed leadership of the debate. Sarcastically referring to Webster and Clay as the "duplicate Senators," he scolded them for criticizing Jackson when the BUS, the most power hungry institution in the country, went its unrestricted way and was about to unleash its financial might to defeat the President in the upcoming election. Benton said he was shocked at the remarks of the Bank men in the Senate because of their disrespect toward Jackson. It was disgraceful to hear the President abused in this manner. Clearly it was part of a vicious campaign to discredit him before the public.[51]

Clay, in reply, laughed at Benton for his present solicitude. He remembered back to 1813, he said, back to a time when Jackson and Benton were not so friendly and had engaged in a gun fight in Tennessee which involved several other men including Benton's brother, Jesse. At least, taunted Clay, "I never had any personal rencontre with the President; I never complained of the President beating a brother of mine after he was prostrated and lying apparently lifeless." Nor, he continued, had he ever said that if Jackson were elected President, Congressmen would have to protect themselves by carrying guns and knives.

"That's an atrocious calumny," cried Benton, springing to his feet.

"What," replied Clay, "can you look me in the face, sir, and say that you never used that language?"

"I look," said Benton, "and repeat that it is an atrocious calumny, and I will pin it to him who repeats it here."

Clay flushed with rage. "Then I declare before the Senate that you said to me the very words."

"False! False! False!" screamed Benton.

Other Senators jumped to their feet, perhaps fearful that

51. Chambers, *Benton,* 184–185.

the two men would attack one another, while the chair gaveled for order. When quiet was finally restored, Benton said, "I apologize to the Senate for the manner in which I have spoken —but not to the Senator from Kentucky." Whereupon Clay retorted, "To the Senate I also offer an apology—to the Senator from Missouri, none!"[52]

So ended round one in what would be a continuing battle over the Bank and over Jackson's expansion of presidential power. And despite the mighty blasts of Webster, Clay and other Bank men in Congress, despite the warning that the President was clearly claiming a controlling role in the legislative process, and despite the fears expressed that Jackson was "entering on experiments with the government and the Constitution," the message held its own. The Congress was unable to override the veto and so adjourned on July 16 to go back and explain to the people what the President had done.

Because there would be a presidential election in the fall, Jackson, in writing his veto, laid the Bank issue squarely before the American people for decision. Never before had a chief executive taken a strong stand on an important issue, couched his position in provocative language, and challenged the American people to do something about it if they did not approve. And the alternative was clear. It was either Andrew Jackson or the Second Bank of the United States.

52. *Ibid.,* 185–186; Ben: Perley Poore, *Reminiscences* (Philadelphia, 1886), I, 144.

4

The Election of 1832

THE PRESIDENTIAL ELECTION OF 1832 was unique in many respects. Not only did it witness the submission of a major issue to the electorate for decision, but it was the first election in which the major parties held national nominating conventions to select their presidential candidates. In addition, it marked the emergence of the first third party in American politics—the Anti-Masons, an extraordinary movement of frustration and anger that had its inception in New York almost five years before.

Anti-masonry began with the murder in 1826 of William Morgan, a stonemason from Batavia, New York. Morgan belonged to a local Masonic lodge and because of a dispute with his lodge brothers wrote a book disclosing the secrets of Free-masonry. Efforts to dissuade him from his treachery failed, so Morgan was kidnapped and taken to Fort Niagara where, according to one source, he was held captive for several days and then drowned in the Niagara River.[1] No sooner did this bizarre story start making the rounds than western districts of New York succumbed to wild excitement. Then excitement yielded to blazing anger as pious, Bible-oriented Yankees who had recently moved to western New York from New England swore to eradicate an order they regarded as a conspiracy of aristocrats threatening public safety and the social order. Determined to eliminate this menace, the agitated citizens of the western counties of the state commenced a political witch-hunt. They crowded into public meetings where they voiced their resent-

1. Thurlow Weed, *Autobiography of Thurlow Weed* (Boston, 1883), 297.

ment. No Masons, they declared, would be supported for a public position, and those already in office would be removed.

While the Anti-Masonic outbreak appeared to some as a democratic movement to terminate the alleged privileges of an elite, to others it was a sudden release of violence produced by the "disturbed and unsettled state of the public mind" during a period of rapid economic and political transition.[2] Unquestionably, deep psychological and religious forces were at work, but even more fundamental in explaining the "disturbed" state of the public mind may have been the economic stranglehold that Albany and New York City bankers exerted over western expansion and speculation. One of the most important institutions controlling western growth was the Mechanics and Farmers Bank in Albany, a company operated under the benign aegis of the Albany Regency, a political machine created by Martin Van Buren to govern New York in his absence. The Regency was a governing council run by such remarkable politicians as William L. Marcy, Silas Wright, Jr., Benjamin F. Butler, Azariah C. Flagg, and Edwin Croswell, the editor of the Albany *Argus,* the party's official newspaper.[3] Their financial adviser was Thomas W. Olcott, the cashier of the Mechanics and Farmers Bank. Not many years later, John Van Buren, Martin's son, told his father, "Now you cannot imagine, without more knowledge of the business transactions of the M & F Bank, how interwoven the prosperity & even existence of the Western Banks in this state are with that Institution." [4] Other "eastern" bankers repeatedly braked speculation in the West for sound business reasons, an action that infuriated westerners. Perhaps, then, the cold-blooded murder of Morgan and the apparent conspiracy to protect his kidnappers unleashed a pent-up fury against all those exercising economic and political advantage in the west. Banks came under very heavy fire from

2. A. B. Hasbrouck to John W. Taylor, March 10, 1828, Taylor Papers, NYPL; Henry Stanton, *Random Recollections* (New York, 1887), 25.

3. Robert V. Remini, "The Albany Regency," *New York History* (October, 1958), 341–355.

4. John Van Buren to Martin Van Buren, February 14, 1834, John Van Buren Papers, photostats in author's possession.

the Anti-Masons, including the mammoth Bank of the United States.[5]

It has been suggested by one historian that the subsequent Democratic attack on the Bank in New York was simply a diversionary move to turn aside the Anti-Masonic assault on the state's own banking system.[6] But this is most unlikely. Why should the Regency have waited three years before initiating this action? Actually they did not attack until after Jackson vetoed the Bank charter, and indeed, even then, seemed reluctant to involve themselves in such a politically dangerous issue. [7]

In any event, the anti-masonic disturbance continued to grow over the next several years and spilled across the borders of New York into Pennsylvania and Vermont and finally into New England and parts of the Midwest. Perceptive politicians such as Thurlow Weed and William H. Seward of New York and Thaddeus Stevens of Pennsylvania quickly recognized the political value of the uproar and directed it into the electoral field. By the early 1830's party machinery existed in several New England and Middle Atlantic states. Then, because both Jackson and Clay, the prospective candidates of the two major parties, were high-ranking Masons, a decision was made to enter the presidential contest in 1832 and run an Anti-Masonic candidate against them. To select this candidate and unite support behind him, it was agreed to call a national nominating convention.

The convention met in Baltimore on September 26, 1831, and represented the thirteen states of New Hampshire, Maine, Massachusetts, Rhode Island, Connecticut, Vermont, New York, New Jersey, Pennsylvania, Ohio, Maryland, Delaware, and Indiana. All told there were 116 members, and included were such distinguished public figures as Weed, Seward, Stevens, John C.

5. Remini, *Election of Jackson,* 138.
6. Lee Benson, *The Concept of Jacksonian Democracy* (Princeton, 1962), 49–54.
7. The Benson thesis that the Regency's assault on the Bank was a diversionary move is well refuted, I think, in Frank Otto Gatell's "Sober Second Thoughts on Van Buren, The Albany Regency, and the Wall Street Conspiracy," *The Journal of American History* (June, 1966), LIII, 36–37.

Spencer, Samuel A. Foot, Henry Dana Ward, Nicholas Devereux, John Rutherford, William Sprague, and Jonathan Sloan. Only New York, Pennsylvania, and Massachusetts had delegations of any appreciable size. Consequently these states dominated the proceedings.[8]

On the third day the delegates nominated William Wirt of Maryland for president and Amos Ellmaker of Pennsylvania for vice president. These nominations, after they were publicized, were generally regarded as boosting Jackson's campaign because they diverted votes that were certainly headed for the National Republicans. Prior to the convention, Clay had hoped to lure the Anti-Masons to his side. "The policy of the Antis," he wrote, "is to force us into their support. Ours should be to win them to ours. . . . I would not abuse them; I would not even attack them. I would leave that to the Jackson party." [9] During the ensuing campaign, Clay coyly beckoned to the Antis, much to the amusement of the Democrats. His advances, laughed the Washington *Globe,* resembled "the advances of an old rake to an honest country damsel." [10]

Democrats, by and large, were heartened by Wirt's nomination. Indeed, Kendall thought it would drive many independents into the General's camp. "We will take care of that in the West," he boasted to Gideon Welles of Connecticut. "You must so manage as to break up the Anti-Masons in your quarter, or at least prevent their union with the Nationals." [11] John A. Dix of New York reported that the Wirt nomination was badly received in his state. "The honest portion of the antimasonic party consider his acceptance coupled with an act of treachery to Mr. Clay, to which they are willing to become accessories by countenancing the traitor." [12] In a further act of treachery toward Mr. Clay, a group of Anti-Masons centered mainly in

8. *Niles Weekly Register,* October 1, 1831; Weed, *Autobiography,* 389.

9. Clay to J. S. Johnson, July 23, 1831, Henry Clay, *Correspondence* (Cincinnati, 1856), 308–309. See also Clay to Francis Brooke, June 23, 1831, *ibid.,* 304.

10. Washington *Globe,* September 8, 1832.

11. Kendall to Welles, September 30, 1831, Gideon Welles Papers, LC.

12. Dix to T. S. Smith, October 20, 1831, Dix Papers, CUL.

New York urged the National Republican party to nominate
Wirt and thereby effect a merger that would hopefully strengthen
their chances of defeating Jackson. But such a merger was quite
out of the question. Clay was the leading contender for the nomination and so "available" to most National Republicans that it
was impossible to displace him. Had it not been for the fact that
Clay was a Mason himself, he most assuredly would have received the nomination of the Anti-Masonic party.

Be that as it may, several leading National Republicans
doubted the strength of the new party. Daniel Webster admitted
that "as a sentiment" the Anti-Masonic movement was growing
rapidly, but as a political organization to govern the nation he
doubted that it had a future.[13] To Webster's mind, naturally,
the only party which could responsibly govern this nation was
the National Republican party. And on December 12, 1831 this
party of responsibility held its own convention in the same
building and same city as had the Antis. Bad weather and
impassable roads prevented more than 130 party members from
arriving for the opening day, although their number increased on
succeeding days until it finally reached 155.[14] In all, eighteen
states were represented, and they unanimously nominated Henry
Clay to carry the party's standard; along with him they chose
John Sergeant of Pennsylvania as running mate. On the final
day of the meeting the delegates listened to an "Address
to the People" and approved its publication and distribution
in the amount of 10,000 copies. Appropriately, the address
flayed Jackson for his failures as President. It said he was "by
education and character wholly unfit" for the office. It scored
his use of the spoils system and his policies toward the tariff
and internal improvements. As for the Bank, continued the
address, this "great and beneficial institution . . . maintaining a sound, ample, and healthy state of the currency may be
said to supply the body politic, economically viewed, with a
continual stream of life-blood, without which it must inevitably
languish and sink into exhaustion. . . . If, therefore, the presi-

13. Webster to Ambrose Spencer, November 16, 1831, Webster
Papers, NHHS.
14. *Niles Weekly Register,* December 17, 1831.

dent be re-elected, it may be considered certain that the bank will be abolished, and the institution which he had recommended, or something like it, substituted in its place."

Did the people know this? And were they ready, asked the address, to sustain such a crushing blow to their economic system? "Are they ready to destroy one of their most valuable establishments to gratify the caprice of a chief magistrate . . . ?" No! Never! It was therefore the duty of every patriotic American to help turn Jackson out of office, and to ease the task for them, the National Republican party had nominated that "statesman, advocate and orator," Henry Clay, an ardent, fearless, and consistent defender of liberty and republican institutions.[15] On that note of ringing enthusiasm, the meeting adjourned.

The first Democratic convention met several months later. In a sense it had a long history because the possibility of a Democratic convention had been discussed by Calhoun and Van Buren as early as 1826 for the purpose of nominating Jackson for the 1828 campaign. Nothing came of the discussion, although the party encountered no difficulty in uniting behind Jackson and Calhoun, his vice-presidential running mate. But after the election, Van Buren and Calhoun fought a deadly battle within the Cabinet over the succession, a struggle that ended in the defeat of the Vice President. Then, to help Jackson purge the Calhoun men from his Cabinet, Van Buren agreed to resign as Secretary of State and take the post of Minister to Great Britain. Congress was not in session when he sailed for England, and not until January, 1832 was his confirmation brought before the Senate for action. Debate on the motion lasted for two days. At the end of it a vote was taken that resulted in a tie, 23 to 23, with Calhoun's friends joining Clay, Webster, and the other National Republicans against confirmation. Thus, the casting vote belonged to the Vice President. Rejoicing "in the opportunity of cutting off V. B.'s head," Calhoun voted to reject the nomination.[16] Still savoring his moment of triumph, Calhoun then turned to a friend and said,

15. *Ibid.*, December 24, 1831.
16. Frederick Whittlesey to Seward, January 25, 1832, William H. Seward Papers, URL.

"It will kill him, sir, kill him dead. He will never kick, sir, never kick." [17]

The National Republicans also rejoiced at Van Buren's defeat. "The late movement in the Senate," enthused one man, "has had the happiest effect in giving confidence and animation to our friends. It has affected them as the capture of the Hessians did the dispirited whigs. . . ." [18] But there was more to the action of the National Republicans than simply the rejection of Van Buren. Apart from their intense dislike of the Magician, the leaders of the party voted as they did to "minister to the personal animosities of Mr. Calhoun" in the hope of winning his partisans into a permanent alliance with the National Republicans.[19]

For their part, the Democrats were shocked and outraged by the Senate's action. "I have an itching to get hold of the d——d rascals that voted against Van Buren," wrote one.[20] Of course Jackson reacted with predictable vehemence. "I have no hesitation in saying that Calhoun is one of the most base hypocritical and unprincipled villains in the United States," he wrote. "His course in secrete session, and vote in the case of Mr Van Buren, has displayed a want of every sense of honor, justice and magnanimity. His votes has dam'd him by all honest men in the senate, and when laid before the nation, and laid it will be, will not only dam him and his associates, but astonish the american people." [21]

It was characteristic of Jackson, who was a close guardian of his fame and reputation, to see the rejection of Van Buren as a personal attack upon himself. "The people will properly resent the insult offered to the Executive," he wrote Van Buren, "and the wound inflicted on our national character, and the injury intended to our foreign relations, in your rejection, by placing

17. Benton, *Thirty Years' View*, I, 219.

18. John L. Lawrence to Clay, January 30, 1832, Clay Papers, LC

19. George Dallas to Roberts Vaux, February 12, 1832, Vaux Papers, PHS.

20. James Watson Webb to Jesse Hoyt, February 12, 1832, Mackenzie, *Life of Martin Van Buren*, 231.

21. Jackson to John Coffee, January 21, 1832, Jackson, *Correspondence*, IV, 400–401.

you in the chair of the very man whose casting vote rejected you." [22] No other reparation was acceptable save the Magician's election to the vice presidency, insisted Jackson. To secure that end and to unite the entire party behind the Van Buren candidacy, Jackson directed that a national convention be summoned in Baltimore in the spring of 1832—not, however, to select a president, but to confirm a vice president, a man already chosen who was 3,000 miles away.

In England, when Van Buren learned of his rejection he was immediately deluged with advice. He finally agreed with his friend Cambreleng that he should do nothing but wait in Europe until after the Baltimore convention before returning home.[23] Not only would it appear in good taste but it would free him from the charge of managing the meeting or exploiting the sentiment in his favor. It would allow the delegates the privilege of "freely" executing Jackson's will.

The Democratic convention met in Baltimore on May 21, 1832. The delegates were either appointed by legislative caucus, state conventions or, in some instances, chosen in city and county elections. A number of party managers showed up at the convention, including Isaac Hill of New Hampshire, John Overton and John Eaton of Tennessee, Simon Cameron of Pennsylvania, and Silas Wright and Azariah Flagg of the New York Regency. In all 334 delegates, coming from every state except Missouri, attended, and on the afternoon of the second day Van Buren was selected as the vice-presidential candidate of the Democratic party. No formal nomination of Jackson took place, although the convention "concurred" in the nominations he had already received from many states.[24]

On Wednesday, May 23, the last day of the convention, the members were instructed to "make such explanations by

22. Jackson to Van Buren, February 12, 1832, Van Buren Papers, LC. Also see Jackson to James A. Hamilton, January 27, 1832, Jackson, *Correspondence,* IV, 403.

23. Van Buren to John Van Buren, February 23, 1832, Van Buren Papers, LC.

24. *Summary of the Proceedings of A Convention of Republican Delegates . . . for the purpose of Nominating a Candidate for the Office of Vice President . . .* (Albany, 1832), 3–8; Samuel R. Gammon, *The Presidential Election of 1832* (Baltimore, 1922), 102.

address, report or otherwise to their respective constituents
. . . as they may deem expedient." [25] It was thought best not
to issue any formal "address to the people" probably because such an address would have to discuss the Bank and that
might cause the party considerable trouble in view of the
Bank's widespread support. So the entire matter was neatly
disposed of by allowing each delegate the privilege of handling
it anyway he deemed appropriate. Then the convention established a general corresponding committee for each state
and a general central committee to reside in Washington. The
delegates adjourned on a note of great anticipation, confident
of their organizing skill to carry the election for Old Hickory.

Indeed, it was the splendor of the Democratic organization that built many of the impressive majorities for Jackson
in all sections of the country. That organization functioned at
every level: state, county, and local, with committees assigned a variety of tasks in order to get out the vote and whip
up excitement for the candidate. For example, clubs were established in most communities to arrange parades and barbecues;
state fund-raising groups were formed to subsidize newspapers
and underwrite the distribution of campaign material; [26] and a
general central committee was appointed in Washington to cap
this organizational pyramid and coordinate the work undertaken
in the several states. [27]

One of the most efficient men in Washington working for
Jackson's reelection was Amos Kendall. As early as the fall of
1831 he had written state politicians urging them to erect a
party structure and reminding them to keep close contact with
the leaders in Washington. "Have you an organization in your
state?" he queried one Connecticut politician. "Whether you
have or not . . . send me a list of names of Jackson men good

25. *Niles Weekly Register,* May 26, 1832.
26. "If our friends in town could help us at this particular crisis, to
about three hundred dollars," wrote one Jacksonian Congressman, "we
will make good use of it." Aaron Ward to Jesse Hoyt, October 12, 1832,
Mackenzie, *Life of Van Buren,* 238.
27. *Niles Weekly Register,* May 26, 1832.

and true in every township in the state . . . to whom our friends may send political information. I beg you to do this *instantly.*" [28]

Another valuable Jackson campaigner was Francis P. Blair, editor of the *Globe.* His sheet spewed out uncommonly good propaganda, a lot of it vicious but all of it hard-hitting and persuasive. When he spotted newspaper defections to the pro-Bank position, he promptly charged bribery and ranted at their editors for their betrayal. After the New York *Courier and Enquirer* reversed its editorial policy and came out in favor of the Bank, Blair described its editor, James Watson Webb, as "That two legged, strutting, mouthing, ranting, bullying animal . . . who has just 'hopped the twig' and now sits perched on the United States Bank, chanting his cock-a-doodle-doos. . . ." [29] Hezekiah Niles, the editor of a Baltimore weekly, was bullied for supporting recharter. The *Globe* noted Niles had "defected to the Bank: *price unknown.*" [30] Congressmen who had borrowed from the BUS and opposed the veto were also charged with bribe-taking. Senators Johnson of Louisiana and Poindexter of Mississippi were accused of accepting $46,000, a charge denied by a sworn statement that these were legitimate loans made for business reasons. All of which proved, said one editor, how low the Jacksonians would swing to gather votes. "*Everyday* occurrences of business are feloniously charged as crimes in individuals." [31] And did the President care? He seemed perfectly content with his editor's performance. He even instructed Major Lewis to tell Blair "that the Globe revolves with all its usual splendor." [32]

Jackson himself boosted the campaign. When appropriate he sent suggestions to party leaders on how the campaign might be conducted. He shrewdly pointed out to Kendall, for example, that an "expose of the members of Congress who have voted

28. Kendall to Welles, September 12, 1831, Welles Papers, LC.
29. *Globe,* September 8, 1832.
30. *Ibid.,* October 16, 1832.
31. *Niles Weekly Register,* October 27, 1832.
32. Jackson to Lewis, August 9, 1832, Jackson Papers, ML.

for rechartering that Bank would have a good effect upon the
public & enlighten the minds of the people in the choice of
Representatives." [33] And he also encouraged subsidies for
Democratic newspapers. On one occasion he went out of his
way to congratulate Secretary Livingston for awarding the
job of printing diplomatic correspondence to the *Globe*. All the
executive departments, he felt, should make this a regular
practice. "It would be mortifying," he said, for such newspapers
to be "embarrassed for the want of that support which the work
of the Departments afford." [34]

Although attendance at public rallies by presidential candidates was frowned upon at this time, Jackson occasionally
showed up at party gatherings to wave to the folks while he was
returning home or traveling to Washington. Whenever he made
such appearances, opposition newspapers immediately pounced
on him. A report that he had stopped off on his way through
Lexington, Kentucky, to attend a barbecue brought a prompt
rebuke from the Washington *National Intelligencer*. "This is
certainly a new mode of electioneering," scolded the editor. "We
do not recollect before to have heard of a President of the United
States descending in person into the political arena." [35]

Like the Democrats, the National Republicans constructed
an efficient party apparatus to win votes. They established
committees, founded newspapers, collected funds, and printed
circulars. And they had one additional advantage: the tremendous resources of the United States Bank. Biddle poured
literally thousands of dollars into the campaign to defeat
Jackson. He paid for the reprinting of speeches by Clay,
Webster, and anyone else who supported recharter. He even
distributed 30,000 copies of Jackson's veto message because he
considered it excellent propaganda for the Bank. Democrats
were rightly terrified by this tremendous infusion of cash into
the campaign. "The U.S. Bank is in the field," wrote the

33. Jackson to Kendall, July 23, 1832, Jackson-Kendall Papers, LC.

34. Jackson to Livingston, July 21, 1832, Jackson, *Correspondence*,
IV, 465.

35. *National Intelligencer*, October 5, 1832.

alarmed Senator Marcy of New York, "and I cannot but fear the effect of 50 or 100 thousand dollars expended in conducting the election in such a city as New York." [36] "The Bank is scattering its thousands here to affect us," reported Isaac Hill in New Hampshire; [37] while another Democrat declared: "I fear the Bank *influence* more than any thing else. I have no doubt that the Bank managers will expend a large sum of money. . . ." [38] Although it can not be determined precisely the exact amount of money the Bank contributed to the campaign, it is likely that something approximating $100,000 was spent by the institution to defeat Andrew Jackson.[39]

This obvious interference in the election by the Bank provided Democratic newspapers with some of its best ammunition. "If the Bank, a mere monied corporation, can influence and change the results of our election at pleasure," cried one, "nothing remains of our boasted freedom except *the skin of the immolated victim.*" As further evidence of the Bank's activities in manipulating the election, Democrats uncovered numerous instances of alleged bribery, not only of government officials but ordinary citizens as well. The "Golden vaults of the Mammoth Bank," said the *Globe,* were opened wide to pay electioneers two dollars a day to campaign against Jackson. Such "bribery" should not go unpunished, declared Blair. "Let the cry be heard across the land. Down with bribery—down with corruption—down with the Bank. . . . Let committees be appointed in every township to prosecute every Bank agent who offers a bribe." [40]

In conducting the War against the Bank, Democrats cleverly broadened the scope of their appeal to embrace larger issues. They spoke of the battle as a contest between Jackson, the people, and democracy on the one hand, and Clay, the Bank,

36. Marcy to Hoyt, October 1, 1832, Mackenzie, *Lives of Butler and Hoyt,* 113.

37. Hill to Hoyt, October 15, 1832, Mackenzie, *Life of Van Buren,* 239.

38. Aaron Ward to Hoyt, October 12, 1832, *ibid.,* 238.

39. For a more conservative estimate see Catterall, *Second Bank,* 265.

40. *Globe,* September 8, October 17, 1832.

and aristocracy on the other. Since this appeal assured a strong emotional response from the unsophisticated, the Democratic press hammered away at it in issue after issue, never relenting, never pausing, never changing the direction of their propaganda. "The Jackson cause," they insisted, "is the cause of democracy and the people, against a corrupt and abandoned aristocracy." [41] Why is the President opposed? asked the Vermont *Patriot*. Because "he supports the interests of the WHOLE PEOPLE—because he will not uphold corrupt monopolies—because he will not become suppliant to the Aristocracy of the land! *This* is why he is opposed. And who are his opposers? Do they class with the farmers and mechanics? No. Do they class with the useful—the laboring men of the country? No. They are the rich—the powerful—the men who grind the faces of the poor, and rob them of their hard earnings. Men who live on their *twenty per cent extortions* from the poorer classes! *These* are the opposers of Andrew Jackson. . . ." [42]

Taking their cue from the veto message itself, Democratic editors tagged the National Republicans the party of the corrupt rich seeking to plunder the honest poor. Thank God, they chorused, the country had a man like Andrew Jackson as its President to stand up to them. "When the Creek Indians, in the late war, began to murder the women and children on our frontiers, General Jackson said, VETO!—*and the murderers ceased*. When Packenham . . . advanced to seize the city [of New Orleans] General Jackson said VETO!—*and the city was saved*. When the company of British Lords and gentlemen . . . [and American aristocrats] asked the government to make them a present of some ten millions of dollars . . . General Jackson said VETO!—*and our liberties and institutions are still safe*." [43]

The bracing effect of this outrageously false propaganda intoxicated Jackson. And he credited it all to the potency of his Bank message. "The veto works well," he told his nephew,

41. *Ibid.*, September 5, 1832.
42. August 22, 1832.
43. *Globe*, October 17, 1832.

Andrew J. Donelson, "instead of crushing me as was expected & intended, it will crush the Bank." [44] Van Buren agreed, though he was a fairly cautious interpreter of the political scene. "The Veto is popular beyond my most sanguine expectations," he wrote; "I will be greatly disappointed if its effect is not very considerable with the great body of people at the election." [45]

To all this propaganda about democracy and aristocracy, the National Republicans countered by nailing Jackson as a despot who understood only three things: spoils, veto, and dictatorship. The Cincinnati *Daily Advertiser* said he had annulled "two houses of Congress, the Supreme Court and the Constitution of the United States." [46] He had inflicted a "calamity on the prosperity" of the nation by his veto, added the *Boston Daily Advertiser and Patriot.*[47] "Could it have any effect but to swell the power and augment the influence of the Executive, but adding money to patronage?" The "Constitution is gone!" wailed the Washington *National Intelligencer.* "It is a dead letter, and the will of a DICTATOR is the Supreme Law!" [48]

As for the attack on the Bank, this was sheer "wantonness," "wickedness," "unmixed depravity" to poison the public mind against a reputable institution with the "grossest charges" that only the "shallowest intelligence" could believe.[49] Newspapers warned that if Jackson was reelected and the Bank destroyed, prices and prosperity would collapse. Already disaster had struck, announced *Niles Weekly Register.* Several hundred persons had lost their jobs on account of the veto, "chiefly mechanics or manufacturers, and many of them heads of families. . . ." [50] An Ohio newspaper cautioned farmers that merchants were offering contracts for pork at $2.50 per hundredweight if Clay was elected, but only $1.50 if Jackson won.

44. Jackson to Donelson, August 9, 1832, Donelson Papers, LC.
45. Van Buren to Donelson, August 26, 1832, Van Buren Papers, LC.
46. August 31, 1832.
47. October 10, 1832.
48. September 6, 1832.
49. *Boston Daily Advertiser and Patriot,* October 12, 1832.
50. September 22, 1832.

"Every man who raises pork loses *one dollar* per hundred by voting for Jackson instead of Clay," pronounced the editor.[51] If the Bank went under, admonished these prophets of doom, prices of corn, wheat, rye, flour, and beef would slump. In addition, "the price of labor and materials must decline as the value of money (because of scarcity) advances—and, with the general balance of trade against our country, the retirement of the bank of the United States must have a powerful and injurious influence over the interests and business of all descriptions of persons, except the brokers and other speculators in money." [52]

This fright campaign paid off. An economic panic, spawned by the uncertainty, lightly brushed several communities across the nation in the late summer and cost Democrats thousands of votes. John Breathitt, the Democratic candidate for governor of Kentucky, told Jackson that a number of counties in his state suffered an economic setback that had had "an adverse" effect upon his election. However, it had since "passed away," explained Breathitt, "and I do not believe that it will injure you in Nov." [53]

Other issues received passing attention during the summer and fall. Spoils, the quarrel with Calhoun, and the Seminole controversy attracted some attention, although none of these commanded persistent attention. Actually there was only one issue in this campaign, and that issue was Andrew Jackson. Democrats had enough sense to realize that the Bank question could sink them so they hid it as much as possible behind the heroic figure of their leader.

One issue, however, had enormous potential for future trouble. That issue was the tariff. The Congress had just enacted the Tariff of 1832 and fears were expressed that South Carolina might nullify it or even secede from the Union. Jackson watched this situation very carefully during the summer, ready

51. Cincinnati *Daily Gazette,* August 18, 1832
52. *Niles Weekly Register,* September 8, 1832.
53. Breathitt to Jackson, August 23, 1832, Jackson, *Correspondence,* IV, 469.

at a moment's notice to dash back to Washington from Nashville and crush the rebellion if it should occur.

Indeed, it was a summer of frights. Aside from the threat
of nullification and civil war, and the predictions of approach-
ing depression, there lurked the presence of a deadly cholera
epidemic. The disease had crossed the Atlantic from Europe
early in 1832 and quickly spread from one American city to
another. By the summer two thousand persons had perished.
"It raged in Philadelphia, terrified Baltimore, threatened Washington, and darted malignant influences in the far West. Cincinnati was attacked, and the troops stationed at unknown
Chicago did not escape. New Orleans had it, instead of the
yellow fever." [54] Henry Clay proposed that the President appoint a day of national fasting, prayer, and humiliation. But
Jackson refused on constitutional grounds, declaring it was up
to the churches to make such a recommendation, not a public officer. Democratic newspapers jeered at Clay for his proposal, commenting that it was most singular for a gambler,
drinker, and duelist like Clay to call the nation to prayer. It was
just an election trick, they hooted. "Could he gain votes by it he
would kiss the toe of the Pope and prostrate himself before
the grand lama." [55]

But Democrats were old hands at election tricks themselves, in fact better at them than the National Republicans. In
a colorful campaign of noise and nonsense, they tried to screen
the unpleasant talk about banks and panics and cholera behind
an organized diversion of parades, illuminations, songs, hickory pole raisings, barbecues, and rallies. Parades and barbecues were the favorites. Near Philadelphia, for example, gigantic
hickory poles were marched through town and planted in the
public square on election eve. "I remember one of these
poles," wrote a foreign observer, "with its top still crowned with
green foliage, which came on to the sound of fifes and drums,
and was preceded by ranks of democrats, bearing no other

54. Parton, *Jackson,* III, 419.
55. Quoted in Charles E. Rosenberg, *The Cholera Years* (Chicago,
1962), 50.

badge than a twig of the sacred tree in their hats. It was drawn
by eight horses, decorated with ribbons and mottoes." Sitting
in the tree itself were a dozen Democrats, waving flags and
shouting, "Hurra for Jackson!" [56]

At another city, some 5,000 persons attended a rally for
the President. "A splendid band of music enlivened the scene,
and a piece of artillery was employed in giving salutes." Then
came several long addresses extolling the virtues of the President, followed by six cheers and shouts of "Huzza for Old
Hickory," "Democracy against the Aristocracy," "Victory."
The rally ended with the singing of "The Hickory Tree," a
tuneful little ditty that cheered on the electorate:

> "Hurra for the Hickory Tree!
> Hurra for the Hickory Tree!
> Its branches will wave o'er tyranny's grave.
> And bloom for the brave and the free." [57]

Night parades were also very popular, and usually more
elaborate. In New York a mile-long procession, lighted by
torches, snaked through the city stopping periodically for songs
and speeches. There were hundreds of banners, all transparen-
cies, on which were inscribed the names of the Democratic
organizations sponsoring the march. After these came huge
portraits of General Jackson, showing him either on foot or on
horseback, followed by pictures of Washington and Jefferson.
Among these banners fluttered an eagle—not a stuffed imi-
tation but a live bird, tied by the legs and perched on a pole
surrounded by a wreath of leaves, just like the standard of a
Roman legion. Then, as far as the eye could see, marched lines
of Democrats honoring their hero. They halted periodically in
front of the homes of well-known Jacksonians where they
rendered a series of lusty cheers and huzzas. They also stopped
at the houses of National Republicans and razzed them with

    56. Parton, *Jackson,* III, 424–425; George Pitt to Buchanan, August
1, 1832, Buchanan Papers, PHS.
    57. *Globe,* November 3, October 20, 1832.

three, six, or nine groans.[58]

The National Republicans also sponsored parades, but perhaps their inventive skill was displayed to best advantage in the cartoons, jokes, and caricatures depicting some ridiculous aspect of Jacksonianism which regularly appeared in the newspapers. One cartoon showed Jackson receiving a crown from Van Buren and a scepter from the devil; another depicted Van Buren as an infant in the arms of the President; a third presented Jackson and Clay as jockeys riding a race to the White House, with Clay half a length ahead. One of the most popular cartoons had Jackson, Van Buren, Blair, Benton, and Kendall all dressed as burglars aiming a huge battering ram at the Bank's front door. Another pro-Bank cartoon showed Jackson as Don Quixote, tilting at one of the pillars of the institution and breaking his lance against it.

By and large, the better newspapers around the country supported Clay and the Bank against the President, their shrill voices caterwauling about the dangers of "Jacksonism." [59] But newspapers, even cartoons, were a poor substitute for torchlight parades and barbecues. As one commentator correctly remarked: "A striking pamphlet can influence voters and so does a well-conducted newspaper; but a hickory pole, a taking cry, a transparency, a burst of sky rockets and Roman candles (alas! that it should be so!) have a potency over a large third of our voters that printed eloquence can not exert." [60]

And it was this hoopla and ballyhoo, organized behind a popular hero, that resolved the election so overwhelmingly in Jackson's favor. The President received 219 electoral votes as against 49 for Clay and 7 for Wirt. Clay won Massachusetts, Rhode Island, Connecticut, Delaware, Kentucky, and a majority of the Maryland vote, while Wirt took Vermont. Jackson captured all the rest except South Carolina which gave its 11

58. Parton, *Jackson*, III, 425.
59. The "spirit of Jacksonism" said the *Boston Daily Advertiser and Patriot*, "is . . . JACOBINISM. . . . Its Alpha is ANARCHY and its Omega DESPOTISM. It addresses itself to the worst passions of the least informed portion of the People." October 22, 1832.
60. Parton, *Jackson*, III, 428.

votes to John Floyd of Virginia. In the popular contest Jackson
received 687,502 votes, and his opponents a combined total
of 530,189.[61] Over in the vice presidential race, Van Buren
gained an easy victory, taking 189 votes to Sergeant's 49 and
Ellmaker's 7. South Carolina awarded its 11 votes to Henry
Lee of Massachusetts, while Pennsylvania gave 30 to its favorite
son, William Wilkins.[62]

Despite the size of Jackson's victory—he received approxi-
mately 55 per cent of the entire vote—it appears that he was
hurt by the Bank issue. Although the number of voters had increased over the previous election, the percentage of Jackson's
popular majority declined slightly from what he had received
four years earlier. He is the only President in American history
whose reelection to a second term registered such a decline.
Thus, despite his vaunted popularity, despite the effectiveness
of the Democratic organization, despite division among the
opposition, many Americans turned away from Jackson after his
first term in office. And many of them did so, not because they
preferred Clay, not because of the scandals that had wracked
Jackson's administration, but because they disapproved his
Bank policy. (Of course, there were also a great many Americans who voted for Jackson even though they disapproved of
his Bank policy. They simply shut their eyes to the issue and
voted for their Hero.) In some communities the financial crisis
brought on by the veto undoubtedly ate into his majority; in
others it was the "scare" tactics of the National Republicans.
As Biddle knew all along, the Bank issue could defeat a candidate, or at least hurt him very badly. What spared Jackson was
the great strength of his party capitalizing on his widespread
personal appeal.

Jackson clearly risked his election, his popularity, and, in
a sense, his position in history on an issue that politically could
do him nothing but harm. He was vindicated by an electorate

61. These figures are not complete nor accurate. They do not include
the Missouri vote for Clay nor complete returns for Clay from Tennessee.
A more realistic set of figures would raise Clay's total popular vote by
several thousand.
62. Remini, *Jackson,* 154.

that trusted and loved him. He, of course, insisted that the people responded so enthusiastically because they approved his veto. But they responded to Jackson, not the Bank issue. If nothing else, the contest proved that Jackson's greatest asset, and perhaps his most outstanding achievement, was his ability to inspire the people to follow his lead, even into dark places that worried and frightened them. Despite their fears, they gave him the support he wanted, providing him with strong popular approval for his second term. Soon newspapers were talking about a third term. "My opinion is," said the defeated William Wirt, "that he may be President for life if he chooses." [63]

"Who but Gen Jackson would have had the courage to veto the bill rechartering the Bank of the U.S.," wrote one man, "and who but Gen Jackson could have withstood the overwhelming influence of that corrupt Aristocracy?" [64] Hezekiah Niles in his weekly newspaper shook his head in despair over the interpretation given the election. What the President had actually done, he said, was exercise "the objectionable and repulsive power of the veto, and cast himself upon the support of the *people* against the acts of both houses of *congress.*" And the people had enthusiastically responded to him. Thus fortified, the President could now go back to the Congress and declare the Bank both "unconstitutional and inexpedient." [65]

In fact, Jackson could do more than that; for in using the election to present an important issue to the electorate for decision he had radically transformed the power base of the presidency. It now rested solidly on the great mass of organized voters. Soon Jackson would go to the Congress and state that because of his election he was the representative and spokesman of all the people, supported by them and responsible to them. With such support he would demand greater authority to direct public policy.

In all the groaning by National Republicans over the out-

63. Parton, *Jackson,* III, 432.

64. George Blair to Willie P. Mangum, December 8, 1832, Shanks, *Papers of Mangum,* I, 588.

65. *Niles Weekly Register,* November 17, 1832.

come of the contest perhaps the most portentous comment of all erupted from the stock market. As soon as the electoral returns were tabulated, the stock of the United States Bank dropped six points—from 120½ to 114½.[66]

66. *Ibid.*

5

Removal of the Deposits

THE ELECTION OF 1832 ended the first phase of the Bank War, a phase that can best be described as a simple power struggle between Biddle and Jackson over recharter. What followed was something else. Shortly after the election, Jackson, again the aggressor, resolved to go beyond the veto and remove the government's deposits held by the Bank, this terminating the financial association of the government with the BUS even before the old charter expired in 1836. And it was with this decision that the War moved into its deadliest phase. The Bank, in self defense, unleashed its full potential to inflict economic misery on the community. Jackson, his will again challenged, went to extraordinary lengths to "strangle this hydra of corruption" once and for all.[1] In no time the War devolved into a disordered contest among politicians and businessmen who scrambled for advantage at the Bank's expense—everyone for himself, pushing for the main chance. This second phase was characterized by intense political and economic jockeying among "men on the make" who were out for anything they could get, each man for himself, snatching at every advantage. But what should be remembered in all this scrambling and jockeying is that the War continued primarily as a political battle, with Jackson calling the shots, and only secondarily as an economic struggle among rising capitalists. Specifically, the President proceeded to exercise even greater control and influence over the operation of the government and the economy now that his institutional powers had been firmly buttressed by mass support.

1. Quoted in John S. Bassett, *The Life of Andrew Jackson* (New York, 1916), 635.

No sooner was the outcome of the election definitely known than Van Buren wrote to Jackson and offered his advice about the next course of action. "The idea of the establishment of *any bank,*" he said, "in *any of the States,* is, I take it, entirely done away with by the veto. . . . My choice would be to make another fair effort to get along without a bank, if experience should shew that one is indispensable to the safe conduct of public affairs, then I have not been able to think of a better allowable course than that which you suggested in substance in conversation when I was in Washington in July viz the establishment of a Bank in the District of Columbia." This scheme, he understood, would leave it to state legislatures to authorize the Bank's operation within their jurisdiction "upon the same terms which are granted to their own citizens or such others as the State Governments may choose to prescribe." [2]

Unwisely, Jackson had not developed plans for an alternate scheme if the Bank were exterminated. In part he was prevented from doing so because of the Nullification crisis which erupted late in 1832 when South Carolina defied the federal government and threatened civil war. There were multiple causes for the crisis. First, the high protective tariffs which South Carolina blamed for the steady decline of cotton prices; second, the growing concern over the future of slavery in view of abolitionist attacks and repeated Negro uprisings such as the Denmark Vesey and Nat Turner rebellions. Thus, when Congress passed a new tariff in July 1832 which lowered some rates but left many essential commodities burdened with protective duties, South Carolina decided the time to act out her anger had arrived. A convention was held in November 1832 which nullified the tariff laws and warned that any attempt to collect the duties would bring secession. For several months there was grave danger of civil conflict, but Jackson in a stunning exercise of political skill brought about a final settlement which included both the reduction of the tariff rates and the repudiation of Nullification by South Carolina. After this compromise was forged, the President took a long political tour along the eastern

2. Van Buren to Jackson, November 18, 1832, Van Buren Papers, LC.

coast to unite the people and dissipate the talk of disunion. It was in the glow of this heady triumph that Jackson, in the spring of 1833, returned to the Bank issue.[3]

The decision to withdraw the government's deposits and place them in state banks probably evolved in the President's mind immediately after his reelection. His reasons for taking the action were obvious. To begin with he feared the Bank's ability to utilize the three remaining years of the charter to upset the verdict of the election and he wanted to reduce its power by denying it government funds. In addition, by escalating the War, Jackson could force greater control over the direction and operation of the government and thereby strengthen his position as President. Also, he could be maddeningly perverse. Hence, the action of the House of Representatives on March 2, 1833, declaring by a vote of 109 to 46 that the deposits were perfectly safe in the vaults of the Bank and should be left there, probably encouraged him to do precisely the opposite. In any event, he first expressed the idea of removal while talking with Francis P. Blair early in 1833. During the conversation Blair complained that Biddle was spending public funds "to frustrate the people's will. He is using the money of the government for the purpose of breaking down the government. If he had not the public money, he could not do it."

As Blair spoke, Jackson became visibly more agitated, finally blurting out the words, "He shan't have the public money! I'll remove the deposits! Blair, talk with our friends about this, and let me know what they think of it." [4]

Blair, always happy to stick another knife in the Bank, readily obliged, but soon discovered that many of Jackson's advisers adamantly opposed the removal of the deposits. Aligned against removal was the entire Cabinet (with the exception of Taney) and such close friends and supporters as Van Buren and William B. Lewis.[5] When Blair reported this information to Jackson, the General greeted it with a gesture of

3. For the Nullification controversy see William W. Freehling, *Prelude to Civil War* (New York, 1966); for Jackson's political maneuvering in the controversy, see Remini, *Jackson,* 130–137.

4. Parton, *Jackson,* III, 500.

5. Wright to James K. Polk, January 21, 1845, Polk Papers, NYPL.

nonchalance. "Oh," he said, "my mind is made up on *that* matter. Biddle shan't have the public money to break down the public administration with. It's settled. My mind's made up." [6]

Kendall, Taney, and Blair undoubtedly played an important role in helping the President make up his mind. Indeed, Kendall admitted later that he and Blair "persistently urged" Jackson to remove the deposits.[7] But in view of Biddle's decision to fight for recharter it is unlikely they encountered any trouble in convincing the President. To Jackson, the Bank was guilty of disrupting the government, challenging his leadership both as President and head of the party, and attempting "to break down the public administration." To reassert his leadership over Congress and the people as forcefully as he knew how, he decided the deposits must come out.

On March 19, 1833, Jackson assembled his Cabinet and read them a formal paper explaining his position and stating the reasons for his contemplated action. He felt the present corporation "under no circumstances and upon no conditions" ought to be rechartered. He also declared that the ground

6. Parton, *Jackson,* III, 500. According to James A. Hamilton, Van Buren opposed the removal of deposits and expressed his feelings to McLane, Cass, and others. Then, in the spring of 1833, when he accompanied the President on his political tour following the Nullification controversy, Van Buren found Jackson "determined upon this most unnecessary and pernicious measure" and therefore changed his own mind. When they returned to Washington upon completion of the tour, Van Buren called upon McLane and informed him of the President's decision and his own "change of opinion." McLane reproachfully replied, "You now advocate the removal in obedience to the wishes of the President." To which Van Buren replied, "I found the President was so determined that I could not oppose him." Hamilton, *Reminiscences,* 258. Amos Kendall tells a different story however. He claims Van Buren sent for him one day and "warmly remonstrated" against the continued agitation for the removal. Kendall gave his reasons for it, but Van Buren maintained his opposition "until Mr. Kendall becoming excited, rose from his seat saying that so certain to his mind was the success of the Whig party in the next presidential election, and the consequent recharter of the Bank that unless the latter were now stripped of the power which the possession and management of the public money gave it, he should consider further opposition useless." The men separated, "both somewhat excited." A few weeks later Kendall met Van Buren, who said, "I had never thought seriously upon the deposit question until after my conversation with you; I am now satisfied that you were right and I was wrong." Kendall, *Autobiography,* 376.

7. Kendall, *Autobiography,* 375.

gained by the veto should be maintained; that if a new bank was chartered it should be one located in the District of Columbia with branches established in those states approving its location within their borders; and that the government should retain the right to appoint the president and as many directors necessary to insure "thorough knowledge" of the bank's transactions. Before recommending such an institution, however, the President desired a "full and fair experiment" in conducting the fiscal affairs of the government without a national bank of any description. What he planned in the interim was a system which would permit him to distribute and deposit public funds in state banks, "at such a time as shall upon a careful consideration of the subject be thought most advisable." [8]

Before the meeting ended, Jackson asked the Cabinet to consider a series of five questions related to these problems and to submit their opinions to him in writing. Put briefly, the questions asked the following: Had anything occurred since Congress last met to doubt the safety of public funds deposited in the Bank? Was the management of the Bank reliable as an agent of the Treasury? If a new bank was established what modifications ought to be suggested? If a new bank was proposed when and in what manner ought the President to communicate his views on the subject? And what system should be adopted for the future disposition of public funds? [9] What is important to note here was Jackson's apparent readiness to continue with another national bank if necessary, a position he never fully abandoned even after the War with Biddle ended.

Within a month most of the Cabinet officers responded to the President's questions, although Louis McLane, Secretary of the Treasury, did not submit his opinions until May 20. Practically all the members of the Cabinet favored the present Bank—except Taney. McLane, whose paper was the most closely argued, opposed the removal of the deposits on practi-

8. Memorandum to the members of the Cabinet, March 19, 1833, Jackson Papers, LC.
9. *Ibid.*

cal and legal grounds. He added that "no system should be established for the future disposition of the public deposites nor any change in the places of deposite of the public money sooner than the expiration of the charter of the present bank may render necessary. . . ." State banks were "generally safe," he declared, but "the experience of the Treasury well justifies the apprehension, that some of them would prove otherwise. Indeed, it is not to be expected that, with the temptations to extend their business which the possession of the deposites would create, with the chance of mismanagement to which such institutions are always liable, and with the hazard of loss to which they are ordinarily exposed . . . a loss should not occurr in some one of all the selected banks. . . ." Moreover, removal was certain to bring the state banks into collision with the Bank of the United States, said McLane. "To the community the consequence of such a conflict could not be otherwise than embarrassing, bringing distress to many and ruin to others. . . . In such a conflict, where the credit and the very existence of the local banks would be in jeopardy, and in such a state of commercial distress as would follow, it would be in vain to consider the public disposites as safe."

"It has been urged against the national bank," continued McLane, "that it would be an instrument of power in the hands of government, to be used for political purposes; and in adjusting the charter of the present bank it was endeavoured to guard against such abuses. The danger of improper influence is, however, as much to be apprehended from the employment of the local banks. Those to whom the power of selection would be confided, could not of themselves possess that particular knowledge of distant or of any local banks which would be necessary to guide them. And in listening to the representations and recommendations of others, it would be difficult, if not impossible to escape error and mischief." At the end of this report, Jackson scribbled in pencil the comment, "There are some strong points in this view—all ably discussed." [10]

10. McLane to Jackson, May 20, 1833, Jackson Papers, LC. See also the letters of Taney, Woodbury and Kendall to Jackson, March, 1833, Jackson Papers, LC.

If the deposits were to be removed as Jackson intended, the Secretary of the Treasury, not the President, had to initiate the action. Since McLane opposed this move—a position Jackson respected though disapproved—it was essential under the circumstances to appoint another Secretary of the Treasury. So, without purging McLane, the President arranged a convenient Cabinet shuffle. McLane was promoted to the position of Secretary of State, replacing Livingston who became Minister to France; and William J. Duane, a leading opponent of the Bank, was recruited as the new Secretary of the Treasury. As early as December 1832, Duane had been queried about taking the post; at the same time, McLane had been consulted about moving up to the State Department.[11] In January Duane indicated his availability, and on June 1, 1833, he assumed his new duties.[12] The fact that Jackson prepared these arrangements the previous December suggests the speed with which he decided after the election to remove the deposits.

By June, Jackson's course was fixed, although he still debated with himself about the time and method of inaugurating a system of deposit banking in the states. As usual he turned to Van Buren for advice, but the Vice President equivocated by offering the opinion of one of his lieutenants, Silas Wright.[13] When Jackson finally summoned him to Washington from New York to participate in the decisions respecting the removal, Van Buren begged off. "You know . . . the game of the opposition," he responded. They will "relieve the question, as far as they can, from the influence of your well-deserved popularity with the people, by attributing the removal of the

11. "It is proper to observe," wrote McLane, "and with a full sense of the kindness and confidence manifested by the President, that some time before the commencement of the last Session of Congress, the undersigned had accepted the invitation of the President to become the Secretary of State, and that the final arrangements for that purpose have been delayed only by the state of public affairs in the interval." McLane to Jackson, May 20, 1833, Jackson Papers, LC.

12. William J. Duane, *Narrative and Correspondence Concerning the Removal of the Deposites and Occurrences Connected Therewith* (Philadelphia, 1838), 2.

13. Jackson to Van Buren, June 6, 1833, Van Buren Papers, LC; Van Buren to Jackson, August 19, Wright to Van Buren, August 28, Van Buren to Jackson, September 4, 1833, Jackson Papers, LC.

Deposits to the solicitations of myself, and the monied junto
in N. York. . . ." [14] This last point had been bluntly expressed by the members of the Albany Regency when Van
Buren asked them for suggestions. Wright warned him that
he would be accused of promoting "some cursed wall street
operation" to ruin the Bank and snatch financial leadership in
the country for New York. [15]

Meanwhile, Duane had hardly arrived in Washington than
he was hounded to remove the deposits. Reuben M. Whitney,
a former director of the Bank turned apostate, sauntered into
his office one day and crudely announced that he was expected
to begin deposit banking immediately. Duane was "surprised
and mortified" by this announcement, particularly since it
indicated "a low estimate which had been formed of the
independence of my character." [16] He protested to Jackson,
and although the President denied authorizing Whitney's visit
he did admit that he wanted the deposits removed. The Secretary kept arguing—more for reasons of pride than anything
else—and returned to the matter on several subsequent meetings. Jackson always listened quietly but invariably ended the
conversation by repeating his wish that the government funds
be placed in state banks. After one such meeting, Duane agreed
that if he could not execute the President's request he would
resign his office. [17]

Because no action had been initiated by the middle of the
summer, Jackson, on July 20, officially instructed Duane to
appoint Amos Kendall as a special agent for the purpose of
finding suitable state banks capable of receiving the government's money. Reluctantly and resentfully, the Secretary complied with this order. As soon as he received his appointment,
Kendall immediately began his search, heading first for Balti-

14. Van Buren to Jackson, September 14, 1833, Jackson Papers, LC.
15. Wright to Flagg, August 8, 1833, Flagg Papers, NYPL. Van
Buren had accepted a plan of McLane's which called for the removal of
the deposits on January 1, 1834, thereby giving Congress an opportunity
to react. But when he learned that the President opposed the plan, Van
Buren quickly backed away from it.
16. Duane, *Narrative*, 6.
17. *Ibid.*, 84–92.

more, next Philadelphia, and then on to New York and Boston. His object was to find bankers not only willing to accept the government's riches but who also qualified as loyal Jacksonians.[18] Kendall was quite explicit on this latter point. In a letter to John Niles asking his views on the banks to be employed in the New England area, Kendall added: "With equal capital and character, those which are in hand politically friendly will be preferred; but if there are none such then we must take those which are in the control of opposition men whose feelings are liberal." [19]

When Kendall returned from his tour he had seven banks to suggest as depositories for government funds: the Union Bank of Maryland in Baltimore, Thomas Ellicott, President; the Girard Bank of Philadelphia, James Schott, President; the Mechanics Bank of New York, John Fleming, President; the Manhattan Company of New York, Robert White, President; the Bank of America in New York, George Newbold, President; the Commonwealth Bank of Boston, John K. Simpson, President; and the Merchant Bank of Boston, Mark Healey, President.[20] With this report in hand, Jackson was now prepared to act, even before Congress convened in December. A more circumspect policy would have dictated delay to permit consultation with members of the Senate and House, but the President rejected this notion because he said that delay would work to the Bank's advantage by giving it additional time "to distress the community, destroy the state Banks, and if possible corrupt congress and obtain two thirds, to recharter the Bank."[21] Instead, he would remove the deposits immediately and then give "a full expose of the reasons that has induced it, and let, thro the Globe, be made, unofficially, a statement of the causes and the facts that has induced it." By proceeding this way, he would "prepare the minds of the people for a full and

18. Kendall to Duane, August 3, 1833, Reports of Amos Kendall Including Correspondence with Banks, NA.

19. Kendall to Niles, October 2, 1883, John M. Niles Papers, CHS. This explains the rationale behind the choice of some non-Jacksonian banks.

20. Letters to Banks, September 26, 1833, Treasury Department, NA.

21. Jackson to Van Buren, September 8, 1833, Jackson, *Correspondence*, V, 182.

official exposure, give strength to our friends, protect the State
Banks, from oppression, and some from destruction, give them
strength by which they can increase their loans to the commercial world as well as to the community at large; and to my
mind this [is] the only step that can be taken to prevent its
recharter." [22]

On September 17, 1833, the President called his Cabinet
together to inform them of his decision and ask for their
opinions. No sooner did Jackson announce his intention than
McLane responded in an "emphatic and lucid manner," artic-
ulating serious objections to the removal.[23] The President then
turned to Duane and asked for his comment. Duane simply
requested that the decision be postponed until Congress convened in December.[24] For his part, Lewis Cass said he would
leave it to the Treasury Secretary to determine, while Levi
Woodbury, the Secretary of the Navy, suggested removal was
unnecessary to safeguard the deposits but that he would accede
to what the President desired. Taney concluded the discussion
by freely admitting he had always advocated an immediate
change and "was now more than ever for it." [25]

Everyone having voiced his opinion, the President adjourned the meeting and asked the secretaries to return the
following day for another session. Jackson's reaction to the frank
comments of his Cabinet is unclear, but he was probably less
than happy over the lack of enthusiasm for his project. When
the Cabinet reconvened on September 18, Jackson opened the
meeting by asking Taney to read an "expose" which he and
the Attorney General had prepared during the summer, detailing his reasons for removal. The paper began almost immediately with a forceful declaration of increased presidential power

22. *Ibid.*
23. Duane, *Narrative,* 99.
24. *Ibid.* This is Duane's version. Levi Woodbury, on the other hand,
claims Duane declined going into the question when asked but chose to
give his opinion at the end of the meeting. Duane felt that because he
was the Secretary of the Treasury his response should come last. Statement by Woodbury, September 18, 1833, Woodbury Papers, LC.
25. Duane, *Narrative,* 100.

by virtue of the recent election. "The President has felt it his duty to exert the power with which the confidence of his countrymen has clothed him. . . . The Bank of the United States is in itself a Government which has gradually increased in strength from the day of its establishment. The question between it and the people has become one of power—a question which its adherents do not scruple to avow must ultimately be decided in favor of the Bank." And it was this power, ruthlessly exercised whenever the Bank chose, that was the cause of Jackson's profound concern. It was the central factor motivating his War against the BUS. Against such growing power what was the electorate to do? "The mass of the people have more to fear from combinations of the wealthy and professional classes—from an aristocracy which thro' the influence of riches and talents, insidiously employed, sometimes succeeds in preventing political institutions, however well adjusted, from securing the freedom of the citizen, and in establishing the most odious and oppressive Government under the forms of a free institution." Again he referred to the Bank's privileges and the constitutional question. He even alluded to Biddle's conduct in the French spoliation claims.[26]

In citing the French problem, the President revealed the extent of his rancor toward the Bank. These claims involved property of Americans destroyed by the French during the Napoleonic Wars. Exerting forceful executive leadership, Jackson had prevailed on the French to sign a treaty by which they would pay 25 million francs in six annual installments. When the Secretary of the Treasury drew a draft on the French government through the Second Bank for the first installment, the draft was rejected because the French Chamber of Deputies had failed to appropriate the necessary funds. In an action more spiteful than wise, Biddle charged the United States government for this default, including principal, interest, cost of protest, re-exchange, and damages at 15 per cent. When the Treasury Secretary refused to pay, Biddle informed him

26. Paper read to the Cabinet, September 18, 1833, Jackson Papers, LC.

that the amount would be deducted from the government's share of the semi-annual Bank dividend.[27] In his paper read to the Cabinet, Jackson called this action "extortion," and another example of Biddle's irresponsible use of power.

The President had also been angered by the Bank's earlier mishandling of the 3 per cents. In March 1832, the government had notified the Bank that it intended to pay part of the national debt in July, an action very dear to the President's heart. Specifically the government planned to redeem half of the 3 per cents amounting to $6,500,000. Since the Bank held the government's money on deposit and was receiving taxes owed the government, it was expected to produce the required funds on demand. However, Biddle was short of cash, having incautiously loaned out a considerable amount of it during the past year despite the advance warning from the Treasury and the fact that he knew the President was committed to liquidating the debt as soon as possible.[28] Embarrassed, Biddle appealed to the government to postpone the payment and received an extension of three months. Later he was informed that the government planned to make a second payment on January 1, 1833, redeeming the other half of the 3 per cents and in effect calling upon the Bank for the grand sum of $13 million within a period of three months. The Bank, through its own miscalculation, now found itself in great trouble. Biddle could ill afford to draw so much money out of circulation, at least not during the 1832 election, so he devised a clever scheme to escape his predicament. He proposed to ask foreign holders of the 3 per cents to pass in the securities (amounting to $5 million) to the Bank which would then hand them on to the government as evidence that the debt was paid. But the Bank would not pay the principal; instead, it would borrow the principal for a year and pay the holders an interest of 3 per cent. To arrange this transaction, which was perfectly legal, Biddle dispatched Thomas Cadwalader to England to consult with the financial firm of Baring Brothers. However, instead of implementing Biddle's scheme, Cadwalader

27. Catterall, *Second Bank*, 300.
28. Bassett, *Jackson*, 627.

concocted something quite different. Because he was unable to convince enough holders to cooperate, he permitted the House of Baring to buy up the 3 per cents for the Bank (paying not more than $91 on $100) with the securities remaining in the hands of the London bankers or in the hands of the original holders.

This arrangement, unlike Biddle's original idea, was in explicit violation of the Bank's charter. The Bank was prohibited from purchasing the public debt, and Cadwalader had specifically authorized Baring to buy the debt for the BUS. Furthermore, by deferring delivery of the 3 per cents the Bank was thwarting the government's declared policy of discharging the debt as soon as possible. Eventually Biddle repudiated Cadwalader's agreement, but only after he was forced to do so by a public outcry. Still he could not understand why there was so much fuss. "Supposing that the certificates are delayed for a few months," he declared, "what harm does that do to anybody? The interest has stopped—the money remains in the Treasury; so that instead of depriving the Government of the use of its funds, directly the reverse is true, for the Government retains the funds and pays no interest."[29] Apparently violating the charter was a trifling matter as long as the government had the use of its funds, according to Biddle. In any event, because of the Cadwalader arrangement, the complete retirement of the national debt was delayed until late 1833.

In discussing the entire incident with his Cabinet on September 18, Jackson said the administration's clear intentions had been deliberately "thwarted" by the Bank, another instance of its power to control government policy. The Bank sent an agent to England, said the President, "for the purpose of preventing the public creditors from doing what they had been called upon by the Government to do. And here the Bank is presented as a Treasury agent defeating the most cherished policy of the Government. . . . If . . . the Bank can already venture to bring in the great Bankers of Europe as its allies in controlling the affairs of this Republic, it appears to the President that a new era may possibly arise in the progress of a few

29. Biddle to C. A. Wickliffe, December 6, 1832, Biddle Papers, LC.

years in which the capitalist abroad may have an influence over the destinies of this country akin to that exercised by them in the States beyond the Atlantic." [30]

When Taney finished his reading of the "expose," the other members of the Cabinet stirred in their seats but had nothing much to say. After a moment or two they silently filed out of the room. Duane hung back until everyone had left the room and then went up to the President and asked if he understood correctly that he was being directed to remove the deposits. Jackson replied affirmatively. Then, in a sudden outburst of emotion as startling as it was unexpected, he began pleading with his Secretary, saying that if Duane "would stand by him it would be the happiest day of his life." [31] In this instant the Secretary realized he had committed a terrible blunder several months earlier in promising to resign if he could not do as the President directed; under the circumstances, however, with Jackson emotionally worked up, Duane could not bring himself to respond so he quietly left the room.

The following day Jackson summoned Duane and asked him if he had decided on a course of action. Hedging, the Secretary informed him that he would give him his answer on September 21. That brought Jackson up sharply. Why did he need more time? It was a simple matter to decide: either do as instructed or get out. A little later, after thinking it over, the President ordered his nephew, Andrew Donelson, to notify Duane that Jackson could not wait until the 21st and that a statement would appear in the September 20th issue of the *Globe* announcing the removal of the deposits. And that was final.

On September 20, as promised, the announcement appeared in the newspaper. No sooner did Duane read the statement than he made up his mind: he would refuse to obey the President's order, and he would not resign.

Unfortunately, Jackson's handling of Duane had been extremely erratic from the start. At two important points during

30. Paper read to the Cabinet, September 18, 1833, Jackson Papers, LC.

31. Duane, *Narrative,* 100.

the disagreement the President had misjudged the situation and got himself snarled in the Secretary's natural sense of pride. The first had come when Duane entered the Cabinet in June. Almost immediately, he felt that he counted for nothing, that men like Kendall and Whitney had more to say about operations in his Department than he, and that he had been brought in to serve as an errand boy. Jackson failed to reassure him completely. The second had come with the *Globe's* announcement of the removal, done without letting him decide for himself what his own course of action would be. Between those two occasions—that is, during most of the summer— Jackson showed Duane great deference,[32] and had he sustained this attitude it is most likely he could have won him over. Instead, now that the announcement was out—with or without his consent—Duane responded to the strong impulse of a badly bruised pride and refused to obey his instructions.

He went to Jackson with his decision. All along the President had believed he had "indulged" his Secretary but that at least when the moment of truth arrived Duane would do as he was instructed or resign.[33] Jackson learned differently.

"But you said you would retire if we could not finally agree," snapped the President after hearing the decision.

"I indiscreetly said so," came the reply; "but I am now compelled to take this course."

The words rasped the old man, but he held tight control of his temper, for he could not afford a quarrel with his Secretary. Should there be an unseemly fight other members of the Cabinet might resign, and a second Cabinet break-up even for a man as popular as Jackson would be a disaster. So the President continued to remonstrate with Duane, patiently repeating his reasons for his decision. The Secretary would not yield.

"A secretary, sir," insisted Jackson, "is merely an executive agent, a subordinate, and you may say so in self-defense."

"In this particular case," responded Duane, "congress confers a discretionary power, and requires reasons if I exercise it.

---

32. Jackson's concern for Duane can be found in Jackson to Van Buren, September 19, 1833, Van Buren Papers, LC.
33. *Ibid.*

Surely this contemplates responsibility on my part."

Duane had a point. The Secretary of the Treasury by law had certain responsibilities to the Congress, such as reporting to it his decision to remove the deposits. What, then, could he do?

Obey the President, declared Jackson, for a Secretary's first and primary responsibility was to the chief executive, not Congress. Still Duane protested, insisting that they must wait until Congress convened.

"How often have I told you," said the weary Jackson, "that congress cannot act until the deposites are removed."

Again Duane asked for a delay—at least ten weeks.

"Not a day," was the stern reply, "not an hour." [34]

Since the Secretary would not obey his instructions and would not resign, the President had only one course of action open to him. Never doubting for a moment his absolute control over subordinate executive officers, Jackson, on September 23, 1833, notified Duane in writing that "your further services as Secretary of the Treasury are no longer required." To Van Buren, the President added, "In his appointment I surely caught a tarter in disguise, but I have got rid of him." [35] As a replacement, Taney was moved over from his position as Attorney General, and Benjamin F. Butler, a member of the Albany Regency and Van Buren's former law partner, was awarded Taney's post.

As careful as Jackson had been in trying to sidestep a quarrel with Duane, this second shake-up of the Cabinet almost precipitated "an explosion" within the official family, for McLane and Cass now felt their positions compromised, their usefulness dissipated, and their resignations imperative. Jackson, concerned over the impact their resignations would have on the country and Congress, exerted all his persuasive skills to get them to reconsider. Cass admitted he had never seen the President "so kind, or more frank. . . ." [36] Jackson assured

34. Duane, *Narrative,* 102–103.
35. Jackson to Duane, September 23, 1833, Jackson to Van Buren, September 23, 1833. Jackson, *Correspondence,* V, 206, 207.
36. Narrative of William B. Lewis quoted in Parton, *Jackson,* III, 502.

him that his confidence in him was "undiminished," that he would regret exceedingly losing him, and that there was not the slightest necessity for him to resign. Both men capitulated to Jackson's strong pleas and agreed to stay at their posts.

Now for the monster! As soon as Taney assumed his duties as Treasury Secretary, he appointed Amos Kendall as special agent for the removal of the deposits. Together, and with the help of Levi Woodbury, they prepared the order of September 25, 1833, which announced the government's shift from national banking to deposit banking. The order stated that commencing October 1, 1833, all future government deposits would be placed in the state banks which Kendall had selected, and that for operating expenses the government would draw on its remaining funds from the BUS until they were exhausted. This "experiment" in deposit banking produced one enormous advantage as far as Jackson was concerned. It gave him almost "complete executive control" [37] in arranging fiscal matters, a responsibility he welcomed since it necessarily removed it from the hands of the Bank. Deposit banking, in other words, represented an enormous extension of executive power.[38]

The "experiment" began with the seven banks, called "pet" banks by opposition newspapers, that Kendall recommended at the conclusion of his summer tour. By the end of 1833 their number had increased to 22. Over the next three years some ninety-odd banks were added to the system, and in each case those selected were considered "friendly" to the Democratic persuasion, or, if not friendly, at least "liberal." By December 13, 1833, the public funds held by the Bank were practically drained away. Because Taney anticipated that Biddle would start a general curtailment in order to force runs on the pet banks and drive them to the wall, Taney sent George Newbold a draft for a half million dollars drawn on the Biddle branch in New York and another $100,000 to Ellicott, President of the

37. Frank Otto Gatell, "Spoils of the Bank War: Political Bias in the Selection of Pet Banks," *American Historical Review* (October, 1964), LXX, 36.

38. Executive discretion in the selection of pet banks was terminated by Congressional action in 1836.

Union Bank of Maryland in Baltimore, to be used only "in difence and to avert injury." [39]

This new assault on the Bank in removing the government's funds represented Jackson's final desperate lunge to kill the Bank outright, to kill it cleanly and swiftly. In taking this action he claimed he had popular support as registered in the last presidential election. And so began a bone-crushing fight between the two antagonists that set off repercussions lasting over a hundred years. To keep his Bank alive, Biddle wielded every weapon in his arsenal, with little regard for the economic suffering or catastrophe he might provoke by using them. After all, he could not be expected to sit idly by while the President hacked his Bank to bits. "This worthy President thinks that because he has scalped Indians and imprisoned Judges, he is to have his way with the Bank. He is mistaken." [40] Biddle demonstrated what he meant by unleashing the full power of his colossus. On October 7 he held a special meeting of the board of directors and won their consent to a general curtailment of loans throughout the entire banking system.[41] He swelled the Bank's liquid assets by refusing to increase discounts and restricting discounted bills of exchange to 90 days. Western branches were ordered to purchase bills of exchange payable solely in eastern cities.

The curtailment order, which some board members objected to, was so sudden that it pitched the country into a financial panic reminiscent of 1819. But Biddle considered it his duty to strike back—and the harder the better. If he brought enough pressure and agony to the money market, perhaps he could force the President to restore the deposits. Then, if the panic persisted, Jackson might be compelled to renew the charter. ". . . The ties of party allegiance can only be broken

39. Letters to Banks, September 28, 1833, Treasury Department, NA. A full discussion of the problems of pet banking, as seen through the operations of the Baltimore pet, is found in Frank Otto Gatell's excellent article, "Secretary Taney and the Baltimore Pets: A Study in Banking and Politics," *Business History Review* (Summer, 1965), XXXIX, 205–227.

40. Biddle to Joseph Hopkinson, February 21, 1834, Biddle Papers, LC.

41. Govan, *Biddle,* 245.

by the actual conviction of existing distress in the community,"
Biddle wrote. "Nothing but the evidence of suffering abroad
will produce any effect in Congress. . . . Our only safety is in
pursuing a steady course of firm restriction—and I have no
doubt that such a course will ultimately lead to restoration of
the currency and the recharter of the Bank." [42]

In brief, Biddle meant to squeeze until the suffering was
unbearable, and in so doing break the "ties of party allegiance"
to win recharter. But this was another foolish mistake on his
part because he was headed for a political fight he could never
win. He could offer little effective leadership, and his action
was bound to cost him popular support. For his part, Jackson
welcomed the fight. "We acted solely on the defensive," he told
Van Buren, "and I am ready with the screws to draw every
tooth and then the stumps." [43]

Biddle's squeeze caught the country at the worst possible
moment. Businesses were undergoing rapid expansion, credit
was needed, the tariff duties came due at this time, and the
demand for ready cash was particularly pressing. In short, a
general prosperity suddenly sustained a crippling jolt. Within
two months the Bank reduced its loans by more than $5,500,000.
In the next five months the total curtailment came to more than
$18 million.[44] Worse, the Bank insisted on regular payments
in specie of all inbalances by state banks. In order to meet this
demand the state banks had to collect from their borrowers and
curtail their own loans. Taney tried to bolster the pet banks to
meet the crisis but they were not strong enough and eventually
had to curtail themselves.

This financial squeeze staggered the commercial and manufacturing centers of the country. Newspapers capitalized on the
alarm and reported a general financial panic in progress; angry
letters swamped Congressmen, detailing the spreading misery.
Dealers and merchants in New York City, reported James A.
Hamilton, "are really in very great distress nay even to the

42. Biddle to William Appleton, January 27, 1834, Biddle Papers, LC.
43. Jackson to Van Buren, October 5, 1833, Jackson, *Correspondence*, V, 216.
44. Govan, *Biddle*, 247; Catterall, *Second Bank*, 321.

verge of General Bankruptcy." [45] "Things are getting worse and
worse here," a New Yorker wrote Biddle.[46] By the end of January the pressure was reported "as great as any community can
bear." [47] Every major city sustained a string of business failures; wages and prices declined; and workingmen were discharged in distressingly large numbers. [48] "Bankruptcy to the
North is almost general," exclaimed Senator John Tyler in
February, 1834, "and where the present state of things will end it
is impossible to say." [49] John Van Buren, the charming and
brilliant son of the Vice President, took it all lightheartedly.
"They say 'the blood of martyrs is the seed of the Church,' " he
wrote, "and heaven knows I have been freely tapped in the good
cause . . . I don't see but I must lose another hunk of my
little earnings." [50] One man who had traveled to Baltimore,
Pittsburgh, Wheeling, Cincinnati, Frankfort, and Louisville
found "great despondency pervading the trading part of the
people." [51] "The distress among the merchants is truly appalling," commented another.[52]

Despite these anguished cries, the stringency was highly
exaggerated. To be sure, a recession had set in, but it was a
minor one and not nearly as severe as businessmen feared.
Nonetheless, popular reaction presumed the recession was a
major economic breakdown; and what men believe rather than
what is objectively true produces panics. "We have never seen
or felt anything like the present pressure," reported *Niles*

45. Hamilton to Van Buren, December 30, 1833, Van Buren
Papers, LC.

46. Charles A. Davis to Biddle, January 27, 1834, Biddle Papers, LC.

47. G. A. Worth to Biddle, January 28, 1834, Biddle Papers, LC.

48. James Van Alen to Van Buren, January 27, 1834, Van Buren
Papers, LC; Catterall, *Second Bank,* 326–327.

49. John Tyler to Mrs. Tyler, February 17, 1834, Lyon G. Tyler,
The Letters and Times of the Tylers (Richmond, Va., 1884), I, 485.

50. John Van Buren to Jesse Hoyt, October 7, 1834, Mackenzie,
Life of Van Buren, 256.

51. Jacob Barker to Van Buren, February 25, 1834, Van Buren
Papers, LC.

52. Jesse Hoyt to Van Buren, January 29, 1834, Van Buren Papers,
LC.

Weekly Register, "and it is becoming every day worse and worse." [53]

Although Biddle was pilloried for precipitating the catastrophe, he was not solely responsible for the recession. Panic conditions probably resulted more from the uncertainty created by the Jackson-Biddle feud than the curtailment itself. True, the squeeze had contracted earning assets and demand liabilities by more than a fifth and inflicted severe injury on business, but the recession itself was a "normal" economic readjustment that might have been expected at this time. To some extent business failures and unemployment would have occurred no matter what Biddle had done.[54]

In any event, and whatever the cause, the recession unnerved Democrats, who were uncertain as to where Jackson's Bank policy would take them. In a country operating under a two-party system, whenever a depression occurs, the party in power suffers the blame and its followers are summarily pitched from office, without mercy and without delay. This was the fear. Moreover, the opposition party had recently shown renewed vigor. Under the pressure of Jackson's removal policy and Biddle's squeeze a new political combination began to emerge in the winter of 1833-34. National Republicans, Bank men, nullifiers, tariff men, states' righters, former Democrats and other dissidents joined together to form the "Whig" party, adopting this name to designate their opposition to concentrated power in the hands of the chief executive. The name may have been first used by James Watson Webb, editor of the New York *Courier and Enquirer,* but it received official sanction when Henry Clay gave it his blessing in a speech delivered in the Senate on April 14, 1834.[55]

So many factions converged into this new party that it is impossible to detect all their reasons for combining. But two things are clear: they objected to the vigorous use of presidential power by Jackson, and most of them opposed his bank policy.

53. May 24, 1834.
54. Jacob Meerman, "The Climax of the Bank War," *Journal of Political Economy* (August, 1963), LXXI, 384, 388.
55. Van Deusen, *The Jacksonian Era,* 96.

They condemned his unwarranted implementation of presidential authority to change an economic system so long established
and approved by Congress and the people. Their newspapers
attacked him as "King Andrew I," a despot of the Old World
plotting to extinguish the freedoms of the New. All through the
winter of 1833-34 Jackson's enemies managed "to get up considerable excitement" both in and out of Congress.[56] They
raised a fearful cry that the country was ruled by a reckless,
lawless, stubborn, ignorant dictator, who would not rest until he
had pillaged the nation of its freedom and liberty.

In Congress the Democrats were panicked by these new
events. They came under heavy attack in the Senate by a triumvirate consisting of Clay, Webster, and Calhoun, who, in
relays, lashed them for blindly following the "tyrant" in the
White House. As this attack mounted in intensity, as the panic
worsened, as complaints from all sections of the country poured
over their desks, as desertions to the Whigs at home were reported, their loyalty to the President and the party was severely
tested. At one point, early in 1834, there was nearly "a breaking up of old parties," reported one Congressman. "The Terrors
of popular displeasure in members from Jackson regions, the
timid, the wavering, the . . . fear of being in a minority at
home, all presented obstacles, that required all our prudence,
forbearance, indulgence, perseverance and spirit to ensure us
success." [57] Rumors swept through the corridors of Congress al-
leging that a majority of House members favored a restoration
of the deposits and that if Jackson did not accede to their wish
his majority in the House would dissolve.[58] Amos Kendall declared that "some of the truest members [of the House] seemed
on the point of yielding." One of them stopped Kendall and cried,
"We cannot resist this tremendous pressure; we shall be obliged
to yield."

"What!" shouted Kendall, "are you prepared to give up the

56. George C. Dromgoole to Edward Dromgoole, January 8, 1834,
Edward Dromgoole Papers, Southern Historical Collection, UNCL.
57. J. S. Barbour to James Barbour, January 22, 1834, Barbour
Papers, NYPL.
58. Samuel Bell to Jacob B. Moore, January 22, 1834, Moore Papers,
HUL.

Republic? This is a struggle to maintain a government of the people against the most heartless of all aristocracies, that of money. Yield now, and the Bank of the United States will henceforth be the governing power whatever may be the form of our institutions." [59]

Though his followers weakened, Jackson was resolute, and increasingly so during the winter because he fancied himself the champion of the people against a "heartless" monied aristocracy. "The President remains inexorable," commented Senator Samuel Bell of New Hampshire, "but many of his partizans are in much distress under the impression that his lawless and reckless conduct and his obstinacy will prostrate the party." [60]

Although the restoration of the deposits was now out of the question—anything connected with Biddle was out of the question—this did not mean that Jackson would not consider the possibility of a new national bank. It is quite possible that he could have been talked into recommending a third bank provided it was politically expedient to do so, provided he was not pressured into it, and provided his "experiment" with deposit banking received a fair trial to see if the nation could successfully adopt to it. An indication of his thinking, particularly in relation to another bank, can be inferred from a series of letters written in 1834 by Benjamin F. Butler, the Attorney General, to Thomas W. Olcott, the chief banker of the Albany Regency. "Let me have in a confidential way," Butler wrote to Olcott in January 1834, "your views as to the best scheme of a new Bank to be located in Washington, with a capital not exceeding 10 millions. You know that though I have always been decidedly & openly opposed to the renewal of the present Bank, yet . . . I have no doubts as to the constitutional power of Congress to create a Bank with such capital & other arrangements, as might be required by the real necessities of the government. I have never found sufficient reason in abandoning this apprehension, & the present state of things is calculated to confirm it." [61]

59. Kendall, *Autobiography,* 416.
60. Bell to Joseph Blount, February 27, 1834, Autograph File, HUL.
61. Butler to Olcott, January 27, 1834, Olcott Papers, CUL.

Butler did not write this letter at Jackson's suggestion, but he was too clever a politician to propose in writing something he knew the President unalterably opposed. True, he warned Olcott not to quote him and admitted he had "no reason to suppose that any plan of a new Bk. at Washington or else where will be suggested or countenanced by the Prest." Still, he recognized that "the present state of things" and "real necessities of the government" might induce Jackson to change his mind. His reason for thinking so was based on the declared policy of the administration as dictated by the President. This policy, he wrote, embraced four points:

1) To dispense immediately with the Bank of the United States.

2) To make use of state banks as depositories of public funds and as agents of the Treasury "to the exclusion, not only, of the *present* Bank, but of *any National Bank,* so long, at least, as to ascertain, with reasonable certainty, whether or not it was practicable, to carry on the business of the Treasury Department, without any such institution."

3) "If it should be found, after a full & fair experiment, that a Natl. Bk was absolutely indispensable then but not till *then,* to examine how far the deficiency might be remedied by the institution of a Natl. Bank, of moderate capital, *at the city of Washington.*"

4) To propose such measures as would ultimately put out of circulation bank notes of small denominations and substitute a specie currency.[62]

Jackson was too realistic a politician to resist the inevitable. He could live with another national bank if necessary. He simply insisted on a fair trial with deposit banking first; furthermore, he did not want to be accused of killing the Bank just to replace it with an exact replica managed by Democrats. Other Jacksonians in Congress also desired a third bank, but many of them were impatient at having to wait out the period of experimentation. There were "more than thirty members" of the House of Representatives alone, reported Congressman Robert T. Lyttle

62. Butler to Olcott, March 20, February 1, 1834, Olcott Papers, CUL.

of Ohio, "who voted with us, & will throughout against restoring the Deposits and also against the present Bank who are *decidedly* in favour of a *New one.*" [63] "Our friends," recalled Congressman Richard M. Johnson of Kentucky, "were divided during the Panic Session upon *the Bank & a Bank.*" [64] This feeling among so many Democrats at this time could produce much mischief, Van Buren told Jackson, and the danger "is not from *the* Bank but from *a* Bank." [65] Still talk continued in Congress that the only way to save the country and the party was to create a third national bank.

But what kind? Here the Democrats ran into trouble trying to decide on a possible substitute. One group wanted a reproduction of Biddle's company but on a smaller scale and under better government supervision. Many of them proposed a $10 million institution located in Washington with other necessary modifications to avoid Jackson's constitutional "scruples." A second group advocated "a people's Bank," in which the stock would belong to the several states and the United States. Still a third group argued for a bank in the District of Columbia that would merely serve as a "fiscal agent" for the government with no power to grant loans.[66] Most of these Democrats were motivated by political or economic fears, or prospects of gain. Besides, they did not believe Jackson's experiment with deposit banking would work. And they were apprehensive over its popular reception. "If State Banks will do," Congressman Johnson explained to Blair, "I am better satisfied than with any National Bank—but if time should not convince the people of this & we all see it I feel confident that you & myself will concur in the course." [67] This was Jackson's thinking precisely.

There were many other schemes for a new bank bruited about during the winter of 1833-34; one was proposed by

63. Robert Lyttle to Francis P. Blair, March 5, 1834, Blair-Lee Papers, PUL.

64. Johnson to Blair, June, 1835 [?], Blair-Lee Papers, PUL.

65. Van Buren to Jackson, July 25, 1834, Van Buren Papers, LC.

66. C. Lawrence to George Newbold, April 1, 1834, Newbold Papers, NYHS; Woodbury to Nathaniel Niles, February 26, 1834, Woodbury Papers, LC.

67. Johnson to Blair, no date, Blair-Lee Papers, LC.

Charles Butler, the brother of the Attorney General, and discussed thoroughly within the Regency. "Mr. Olcott was very
much pleased with my plan," reported young Butler to Silas
Wright, "& was very anxious that I should hurry it to Washington & urge it & he called a meeting of a number of gentlemen &
discussed the subject." What he proposed was the creation of an
office of Exchange and Currency located in Washington with a
capital of $10 million and "the power to discount & deal in do-
mestic bills of exchange." Its paper would be limited to $20
million, and limited also in the denomination of its bills. The
Exchange office would have the right to locate an agency in
any state, provided it first received the "advice and consent" of
the legislatures of the states involved.[68]

The mention of limiting the denomination of bills recalled
point four of Jackson's policy outlined by the Attorney General
in his letter to Olcott. It was a hope the President had cherished
for years. Put simply, Jackson wanted the deposit banks to
cease issuing or receiving bank notes under five dollars. Later,
in easy stages, they were to prohibit notes under ten dollars,
then under twenty dollars, and in this way restore the nation to
specie currency.[69]

Jackson's hard money scheme had the powerful support in
Congress of Senator Benton—"Old Bullion" they called him—
who, like the President, insisted on gold and silver as the circulating medium of exchange. So closely was the Senator's name
associated with specie that some people referred to gold and
silver coins as "Benton mint-drops." [70] Both Jackson and Benton believed that an elimination of paper money, at least under
twenty dollars, would help restore the country to the virtues of
"plain republicanism" and yet it would not interfere with businessmen pursuing their legitimate economic interests. Under a
paper system, according to hard money men, the country was
saddled with boom or bust financial cycles. When the economy
boomed, creditors were rewarded with exorbitant profits on

68. Charles Butler to Wright, February 10, 1834, Butler to—,
March 12, 1834, Charles Butler Papers, LC.
69. Butler to Olcott, March 20, 1834, Olcott Papers, CUL.
70. Poore, *Reminiscences,* 133.

their investments; but when a bust resulted, credit disappeared and the working classes had no money with which to pay their debts, thus losing their property and spiraling the nation deeper into depression.[71]

Jackson's ideas about specie was another shattering experience for Democrats. It was bad enough to refuse recharter, worse to remove the deposits, but this fantastic money scheme seemed too much. Benjamin Butler tried to reassure the Regency. "In respect to the *hard money* proposition," he wrote Olcott, "which I perceive has excited some apprehension among our friends who are interested in the local Banks, I . . . assure you that he [the President] entertains no such Utopian dreams as the opposition presses have ascribed to him. If he were enabled to regulate the whole matter precisely as he could wish, he would proceed to higher amounts, but not ultimately to an amount higher than $20. If there are any person who wish to go further, it is enough to say that their number is not only very small, but that there is not the slightest *possibility* of carrying any such project into effect." [72]

The confusion of the Democrats in Congress was immediately apparent when the so-called "Panic session" began in December, 1833. Although the Jacksonians had a majority in the House of Representatives, it seemed constantly on the verge of breaking up. In the Senate the Democrats were outnumbered, and suffered the additional disadvantage of facing three powerful guns in Henry Clay, Daniel Webster, and John C. Calhoun. Almost immediately the Congress became the scene of a ferocious verbal duel between the banking and anti-banking forces that finally necessitated presidential interference to prevent a complete Democratic rout.

The session began badly for the President. Trouble erupted almost as soon as Jackson sent down his annual message and Taney submitted his Treasury report justifying the removal of the deposits. The President expected Taney's report to be forwarded to the House Ways and Means Committee, chaired by the Democratic floor leader, James Knox Polk of Tennes-

71. *Register of Debates,* 23rd Congress, 1st Session, 1073–1105.
72. Butler to Olcott, March 20, 1834, Olcott Papers, CUL.

see. Polk and the other members of the committee could be counted on to treat the report lovingly and return a set of resolutions to the full House approving the removal. However, George McDuffie, acting on the suggestion of Clay, requested that Taney's report be taken up not by the Ways and Means Committee but by the committee of the whole, and Polk carelessly let himself be trapped by the request. Once the request was approved, McDuffie then proposed unlimited discussion of whether or not the President had the authority to remove the deposits, a debate the Democrats fervently sought to avoid.

Jackson sagged with disappointment over the incredibly bad management of his friends in the House. Repeatedly, he shot letters to Polk telling him that the "time for full discussion is when the committee collect the facts and report them to the House." [73] This was perfectly obvious, and Polk, in reply, could do nothing but complain that he had been tricked.[74]

Under presidential prodding, Polk maneuvered to force the House to reconsider its decision to refer Taney's message to the committee of the whole, but this motion was debatable and debate could not be terminated except by passing the previous question, always a difficult procedure. Nevertheless, Polk tried his luck and was defeated by three votes. Unbelievable as it was, the Democratic leaders could not control the proceedings in the House where they enjoyed a majority. By their gross mismanagement they played straight into the hands of the Whigs and permitted a debate to develop which gave the Bank men a public forum to alarm the nation about the dangers of the President's financial policies. The protracted debate also weakened the Jacksonian party, for on several motions to refer certain banking questions to the Ways and Means Committee, the House leaders had difficulty holding the Democrats in line. On at least one occasion it looked as though a general stampede away from the President was imminent. Democratic confusion

73. Jackson to Polk, December 18, 1833, Jackson, *Correspondence*, V, 234.
74. Charles G. Sellers, *James K. Polk, Jacksonian* (Princeton, 1957), 215.

and unrest worsened during the winter as petitions and memorials favoring the Bank swamped the Congress, further straining "the ties of party allegiance." [75]

Over in the Senate things were just as bad, if not worse. There the speeches were particularly acrimonious, with Jackson verbally assaulted almost every day of the session. The debate in the upper house centered around two vital points: whether the President could assume control of the public treasury, and whether the Secretary of the Treasury was an officer of the executive or legislative departments, subject to the authority of the President or Congress. On the latter point many in Congress argued long and effectively against executive control. Henry Clay led the forces in denying that the Secretary of the Treasury was subject to the President. This particular Secretary, said Clay, had duties "which were exclusively legislative in their character, and which the Executive had no control over." [76] However, it was one of Jackson's lesser contributions that by the time his administration ended, he forced a general recognition that all Cabinet officers functioned under the authority and direction of the President and could be removed by him at will.

Clay started the fireworks in the Senate on December 10 by offering a resolution requesting that the President lay before the upper house the document he had read to his Cabinet just prior to the removal. Quite properly and not unexpectedly, Jackson refused the request as an invasion of his executive prerogatives, whereupon Clay pounced on the refusal as an excuse to introduce two resolutions into the Senate: the first censured Jackson for the removal of the deposits as a misuse of presidential power, the second declared the reasons offered by Taney for the removal as "unsatisfactory and insufficient." [77] But the object of these resolutions was not to demonstrate senatorial displeasure in order to recall presidential action. According to Senator Benton, they were introduced "purely and simply for

75. Biddle to William Appleton, January 27, 1834, Biddle Papers, LC.

76. *Register of Debates*, 23rd Congress, 1st Session, 1175.

77. *Ibid.,* 58, 220.

popular effect. Great reliance was placed upon that effect. It was fully believed . . . that a senatorial condemnation would destroy whomsoever it struck—even General Jackson." [78]

In his speech supporting the resolutions, Clay accused the President of "open, palpable and daring usurpation." It was not a financial problem that caused him to speak out, not a matter of banks and charters and money, but the rapaciousness of the Executive in seeking to expand the powers of his office. "We are," he said, "in the midst of a revolution, hitherto bloodless, but rapidly tending towards a total change of the pure republican character of the Government, and the concentration of all power in the hands of one man." The President had paralyzed the powers of Congress through "an extraordinary exercise of the executive veto, not anticipated by the founders of the constitution, and not practiced by any of the predecessors of the present Chief Magistrate."

But something besides the veto bothered Clay. It was the assertion heard repeatedly since the election that Jackson's authority to act in removing the deposits came directly from the people by virtue of his victory at the polls. This is utter nonsense, cried Clay. "Sir," he said, "I am surprised and alarmed at the new source of executive power which is found in the result of a presidential election. I had supposed that the constitution and the laws were the sole source of executive authority . . . that the issue of a presidential election was merely to place the Chief Magistrate in the post assigned to him. . . . But it seems that if, prior to an election, certain opinions, no matter how ambiguously put forth by a candidate, are known to the people, those loose opinions, in virtue of the election, incorporate themselves with the constitution, and afterwards are to be regarded and expounded as parts of the instrument!"

Clay closed his speech with an emotional wallop that had the spectators in the galleries on their feet, cheering and clapping their hands. "The premonitory symptoms of despotism are upon us," he said; "and if Congress do not apply an instantaneous and effective remedy, the fatal collapse will soon come on, and we shall die—ignobly die—base, mean, and abject slaves;

78. Benton, *Thirty Years' View*, I, 423.

the scorn and contempt of mankind; unpitied, unwept, un-
mourned!" [79]

Clay's speech blooded the battle line. When it was shown to
Jackson the old man's temper blazed up on all its magnificent
fury. "Oh, if I live to get these robes of offiice off me," he
seethed, "I will bring the rascal to a dear account." [80] He likened
the Senator to "a drunken man in a brothel," reckless, destruc-
tive, and "full of fury." [81]

As the debate in the Senate over executive usurpation
mounted in vituperation and insult, Martin Van Buren, the
presiding officer, pretended not to hear the devastating attacks on his friend. But at one point Clay demanded his attention. In a voice soaring with sarcasm, he implored the Vice
President to go to the White House and on bended knee "exert
his well-known influence" over the President and insist upon
the restoration of the deposits. When this demonstration of bad
taste and bad manners ended, Van Buren gestured another
Senator into his seat as presiding officer and hopped down to
the floor. He then walked straight across the chamber toward
Clay. It suddenly seemed that a brawl was about to occur on the
floor of the Senate between the Vice President of the United
States and the nation's most distinguished Senator. Seeing Van
Buren close in on him, Clay slowly rose from his seat. He
stared ahead, watching in fascination as the figure came steadily
toward him. Spectators held their breath, not knowing what to
expect. At last Van Buren reached Clay's side, but instead of
rebuking the Senator with some violent action or demanding
satisfaction in the name of his maligned friend, he bowed. Then,
in a mocking voice, he said, "Mr. Senator, allow me to be in-
debted to you for another pinch of your aromatic Maccoboy."
The words snapped the tension and the Senate breathed a sigh
of relief as Clay waved his hand toward the gold snuff-box he
had on his desk. Van Buren took a pinch of the snuff, applied it
to each nostril and then leisurely returned to the Vice Presi-

79. *Register of Debates,* 23rd Congress, 1st Session, 84–85, 94.

80. Parton, *Jackson,* III, 542.

81. Jackson to Andrew Jackson, Jr., February 16, 1834, Jackson,
Correspondence, V, 249.

dent's chair, almost winking at Senators as he went.[82]

Clay's denunciation of executive despotism was buttressed by Webster and Calhoun in heroic speeches that took days to deliver. Calhoun was still suffering from the whipping Jackson had given him over the Nullification controversy, and in his speech he indicated that the stripes still pained. Compared to Jackson, he said, Caesar was a virtuous statesman when he plundered the Roman treasury. At least his pillage was done openly like a bold warrior. "The actors in our case," he rumbled, "are of a different character—artful, cunning, and corrupt politicians, and not fearless warriors. They have entered the treasury, not sword in hand, as public plunderers, but, with the false keys of sophistry, as pilferers, under the silence of midnight." [83]

This organized grinding of the President was answered by equally lengthy and intemperate speeches by Democrats, most notably by Benton and John Forsyth of Georgia. Benton took four days to cut up Clay. He returned sarcasm for ridicule, stinging rejoinder for biting accusation. "The senator from Kentucky," sneered Benton, "calls upon the people to rise, and drive the Goths from the capitol. Who are those Goths? They are General Jackson and the democratic party—he just elected President over the senator himself, and the party just been made the majority in the House—all by the vote of the people. It is their act that has put these Goths in possession of the capitol to the discomfiture of the senator and his friends; and he ought to be quite sure that he felt no resentment at an event so disastrous to his hopes, when he has indulged himself with so much licence in vituperating those whom the country has put over him." [84] In passing, he pointed out that the censure motion in effect charged the President with an impeachable offense, a matter for the House to consider, Benton said, not the Senate.

Benton's lambasting of Clay drew an appreciative response from Jackson. "Say to [Benton]," the President instructed Lewis, "the people soon will vote him a golden medal for his

82. Stanton, *Random Recollections,* 205–206.
83. *Register of Debates,* 23rd Congress, 1st Session, 220.
84. Benton, *Thirty Years' View,* I, 409.

conduct in the Senate." [85] Indeed so excellent were his services against the Bank forces all during the War that Attorney General Butler told his wife that it was the combined energy of Jackson in the White House and Benton in the Congress that eventually pulled down the Bank. They were "the chief destroyers of the *monster,*" Butler declared. "I found old Bullion hard at work." [86]

What really infuriated the Whigs as the Senate debate grew hotter was the point mentioned earlier by Clay, namely the repeated Democratic argument that Jackson had somehow achieved a popular basis for action, that because the President had taken the Bank issue to the people and won reelection he had acquired new authority. Speaking for most Whigs, Senator Peleg Sprague of Maine denied any such authority. "We are told," he said, "and it is constantly reiterated in our ears, that in all these assumptions and claims of prerogative, the President is sustained by the people. . . . But they [the people] are not infallible." They are prone to idolatry. "And oftentimes a military chieftain, having wrought real or fancied deliverance by successful battles," becomes the object of this idolatry. "In the proxysm of their devotion they are ready at his shrine to sacrifice their rights, their liberties, their children and themselves." [87]

Democrats countered by ridiculing Whig willingness to approve the power exercised by the BUS, which owed no responsibility to the people, but condemned the exercise of presidential power, augmented by popular support.[88] Yet despite these Democratic arguments and despite the powerful declamations of Benton and Forsyth, the Jacksonians could not dissolve the Whig majority in the Senate, and that majority was out to get the President. So, on February 5, 1834, the second resolution that rejected Taney's reasons for the removal of the deposits was jammed through the Senate by a vote of 28 to 18; and on March 28, the censure resolution passed the same body by the vote of 26 to 20. Adding injury to insult, the Senate, late in the session,

85. Jackson to Lewis, July 26, 1834, Jackson-Lewis Papers, NYPL.
86. Butler to Harriet Butler, 1834, Butler Papers, NYSL.
87. *Register of Debates,* 23rd Congress, 1st Session, 386–387.
88. See, for example, Senator Isaac Hill's speech in *ibid.,* 791.

also rejected the nomination of Taney as Secretary of the Treasury.

The censure was a savage blow to Jackson's pride. Always the guardian of his own fame, and ever the defender of presidential privileges, he seemed crushed by the Senate's action. But not for long. Stung by the hurt of the censure, he stirred himself and soon fired back a "Protest" at the Senate written by Taney, Kendall, and Butler claiming the resolution utterly incompatible with the "spirit of the Constitution and with the plainest dictates of humanity and justice." "So glaring were the abuses and corruptions of the bank," Jackson wrote, ". . . so palpable its design by its money and power to control the Government and change its character, that I deemed it the imperative duty of the Executive authority . . . to check and lessen its ability to do mischief. . . . The resolution of the Senate . . . presupposes a right in that body to interfere with this exercise of Executive power. If the principle be once admitted, it is not difficult to perceive where it will end. If by a mere denunciation like this resolution the President should ever be induced to act . . . contrary to the honest convictions of his own mind in compliance with the wishes of the Senate, the constitutional independence of the executive department would be . . . effectively destroyed and its power . . . transferred to the Senate. . . ."

In addition, Jackson reminded the Congress that its legislative power was subject to his veto, though of course they could override it if they could muster sufficient votes in both houses; that the executive power was vested *exclusively* in the President; that the power of appointing, controlling and removing those who executed the laws belonged to the chief executive; that the custody of public property and money was a function of the executive department; that the Secretary of the Treasury was subject to the "supervision and control" of the President; and that the law establishing the BUS could not change the relation between the President and his Secretary.

In accordance with "a solemn decision of the American people" expressed in the recent election (Jackson never failed to make this point again and again) and in view of the "ex-

posed abuses and corruptions" in the Bank, the President said
he had directed the Secretary of the Treasury to remove the deposits. The Secretary did not concur in that opinion, so he was
dismissed and replaced by one whose "opinions are well known
to me. . . ."

Jackson then formally proclaimed what had been implicit in
many of his previous messages. "The President," he declared,
"is the direct representative of the American people. . . ."
He did not attempt a full exposition of this novel doctrine
except to say that Cabinet officers became responsible to the
people only because they were subordinate to the chief executive. Thus, if the Secretary of the Treasury was in fact independent of the President in the execution of the laws, as the
Whigs contended, then there is "no direct responsibility to the
people in that important branch of the Government. . . ." It
means that the Secretary can defy "the Chief Magistrate
elected by the people and responsible to them. . . ." [89]

Responsible to the people! That statement jolted the Whigs.
First, Jackson claimed that his power to act had been enlarged as a result of his popular victory at the polls. Next, he
said he was the direct representative of the people. And now, he
added the final touch by asserting a responsibility to the electorate. Where was it written in the Constitution or the laws,
asked the Whigs, that the President was responsible to the
people? Obviously, Jackson was embarked on another adven-
ture to weaken the power of the Congress by denying the tie of
responsibility between the President and the Congress. There was
no such responsibility as he claimed, they thundered, no such
relationship. Still, with all this criticism leveled at him, Jackson
had forcefully established his major points: that he, as President, was the tribune of the people (implying at the same time
that the Congressmen were not) and that he was directly
responsible to them for this actions.

The "Protest" was a bold and vigorous statement of presidential prerogatives and independence. Strongly worded and
tightly argued, it was a clear declaration that Jackson intended to

89. Richardson, *Messages and Papers,* II, 1295, 1298, 1301, 1304,
1305, 1309.

protect his office from Congressional encroachment. But he did not stop there. Ever the shrewd politician, he reached beyond the Senate and addressed himself directly to the American people, informing them that this conspiracy against the presidential office was really an attack upon democracy and freedom. All he had tried to do, he asserted, was "return to the people unimpaired the sacred trust they have confided to my charge; to heal the wounds of the Constitution and preserve it from further violation; to persuade my countrymen, as far as I may, that it is not in a splendid government supported by powerful monopolies and aristocratical establishments that they will find happiness or their liberties protection, but in a plain system, void of pomp, protecting all and granting favors to none, dispensing its blessings, like the dews of Heaven, unseen and unfelt save in the freshness and beauty they contribute to produce. It is such a government that the genius of our people requires, such an one only under which our States may remain for ages to come united, prosperous and free." [90]

Here was Jackson at his political best, appealing directly to the people and arguing a defense against privilege and wealth. This was his special style; for no matter the issue he invariably carted it before the people and equated it in terms of democracy, which he represented, against an aristocracy, represented by his enemies. Whether right or wrong, he presumed popular approval. And, put to the test, that approval was inevitably given. It was not surprising, therefore, that he believed and preached that as President he functioned as the sole elected official of the entire nation and was responsible to the nation for his actions. He had been placed in office to protect the country's interests; if, in time, the people felt he abused his position, violated their interests or misrepresented their will, then they could replace him with someone else.

The "Protest" constituted a most dangerous challenge to the Whig theory of legislative government. As such it could not go unanswered. Since Daniel Webster was now regarded as "The Great Expounder and Defender of the Constitution" [91]

90. *Ibid.*, 1312.
91. Poore, *Reminiscences,* 146.

he was expected to pulverize Jackson's entire position. Rising
in the Senate to carry out his assignment, Webster attacked all
the major points of Jackson's argument. He denied "that the
whole executive power is in the President"; he criticized Jackson's removal policy as an expression of executive usurpation; and he rejected the argument that the members of the
Cabinet fell under the absolute control of the President. Jackson
"calls the Secretaries *his* Secretaries," mocked Webster, "not
only once, but repeatedly." What an "astounding assertion,"
he went on. Translated, it means simply this: "ONE RE-
SPONSIBILITY, ONE DISCRETION, ONE WILL!"

As to the President's statement about his responsibility to
the people, perhaps the most offensive of his claims, Webster
had nothing but contempt. "Again and again we hear it said
that the President is responsible to the American people! that
he is responsible to the bar of public opinion! For whatever he
does, he assumed accountability to the American people! . . .
And this is thought enough for a limited, restrained, republican government! An undefined, undefinable, ideal responsibility
to the public judgment!" Webster paused, his features darken-
ing by the intensity of his feelings. "I ask again, Sir," he continued. "Is this legal responsibility? Is this the true nature of a
government with written laws and limited powers?"

Then Webster confronted Jackson's novel concept that the
President is the tribune of the people. Again, he denied the
contention. "Connected, Sir, with the idea of this airy and
unreal responsibility to the public is another sentiment, which
of late we hear frequently expressed; and that is, *that the
President is the direct representative of the American people.*
This is declared in the Protest in so many words. . . . Now,
Sir, this is not the language of the Constitution. The Constitution nowhere calls him the representative of the American
people; still less their direct representative. It could not do so
with the least propriety." The obvious proof was the mode of
presidential elections. "He is not chosen directly by the people,
but by a body of electors," argued the Senator, "some of whom
are chosen by the people, and some of whom are appointed
by the State legislatures. Where, then, is the authority for

saying that the President is the *direct representative of the People?* . . . I hold this, Sir, to be a mere assumption, and dangerous assumption." Seeing the many nods of approval from several Whigs in the chamber, Webster concluded with a vigorous rejection of Jackson's entire theory. "And if he may be allowed to consider himself as the SOLE REPRESENTATIVE OF ALL THE AMERICAN PEOPLE," the Senator stormed, "then I say, Sir, that the government (I will not say the people) has already a master. I deny the sentiment, therefore, and I protest against the language; neither the sentiment nor the language is to be found in the Constitution of this Country." [92]

Webster gained strong vocal support on this point from John C. Calhoun. The two Senators may have had their constitutional differences on other matters, but concerning the President's interpretation of his relation to the electorate they were agreed. Speaking before a crowded Senate and gallery, Calhoun said: Jackson "tells us again and again, with the greatest emphasis, that he is the immediate representative of the American people. He the immediate representative of the American people!. . . What effrontery! What boldness of assertion! The immediate representative! Why, he never received a vote from the American people. He was elected by electors . . . and of course is at least as far removed from the people as the members of this body, who are elected by Legislatures chosen by the people."

Calhoun ventured to explain Jackson's purposes in making his extraordinary claims. "Why all this solicitude on the part of the President to place himself near the people . . . ? Why this solicitude to make himself their sole representative . . . ? The object cannot be mistaken. It is preparatory to further hostilities—to an appeal to the people . . . to enlist them as his allies in the war which he contemplates against this branch of the Government." [93]

Other Senators contended that Jackson's position violated the explicit language of the Constitution, particularly his argu-

92. Daniel Webster, *The Writings and Speeches of Daniel Webster* (Boston, 1903), VII, 139, 143, 144, 145, 147.

93. *Register of Debates,* 23rd Congress, 1st Session, 1646.

ment about responsibility. In foreign affairs, they pointed out, the chief executive must not only seek the advice of the Senate but also its consent. Was this not clear proof that the President's responsibility was directly to Congress?

In his turn, Henry Clay condemned the "Protest" as just another form of the veto. Arguing that Jackson had cleverly developed six variations of the veto, almost all of them unconstitutional, Clay said the "Protest" was an "initiatory veto" wherein before legislative action is even prepared for the President's consideration he notifies Congress of his displeasure and in that way initiates the kind of legislation he wants. Jackson claims to be "the sole Executive," said Clay, "all other officers are his agents, and their duties are his duties. . . . I deny it absolutely," declared the Senator. "There exists no such responsibility to the President. All are responsible to the law. . . ." [94]

Despite the hammer-like blows of the Whig leaders in their attempts to discredit Jackson's novel concept, the idea that the President directly represented the people and was responsible to them found ready acceptance with the electorate. Perhaps Jackson intuitively knew this would happen; perhaps that explains why he did not attempt an elaborate defense of the idea in his "Protest." He just shot it out—simply, forcefully. And the people offered no resistance to the concept, much to the regret of Webster, Clay and Calhoun. Obviously the time was right for its acceptance, and eventually even the Whigs capitulated to it. Sighed Senator Benjamin W. Leigh of Virginia: "Until the President developed the faculties of the Executive power, all men thought it inferior to the legislature—he manifestly thinks it superior; and in his hands the monarchial part of Government (for the Executive is monarchial . . .) has proved far stronger than the representatives of the States. . . ." [95]

In introducing and ultimately forcing acceptance of his doctrine, Jackson liberated the President from the position of prime minister, responsible only to the Congress. In effect he altered the essential character of the presidency. No longer

94. *Ibid.*, 1575.
95. *Ibid.*, 1375.

was the chief executive simply the head of a coordinate branch
of the government; no longer was he restricted in his actions
by what he could maneuver from the legislature. Henceforth
he could assert himself as the spokesman of the people and by
the skillful use of his powers force Congress to follow his lead.
This did not free him from the political necessity of working
with Congress to accomplish the public will, but it did allow
him to assume greater control of the government and to
dominate and direct public affairs.

No one articulated this doctrine more clearly than Jackson;
no one pressed it more consistently nor established it more
firmly as part of the American system of government. As Calhoun said, Jackson repeated the doctrine to "us again and again,
with the greatest emphasis." Eventually he got the message
across, despite heavy opposition. His achievement, therefore,
represented a major victory. The first modern President, as
that term is generally understood, Jackson used his office for
purposes of national leadership. He strengthened the presidency, redefined its role, and profoundly altered its relationship
to the people. Said Clay: Andrew Jackson "is the greatest
latitudinarian that has ever filled the office of President." [96]

Despite the President's claims, some Democrats tried to
convince him that the masses thought differently than he about
the Bank and that his pursuit of the BUS did not represent the
popular will. But when such claims were argued, Jackson invariably replied that the Democrats were confusing the people
with the aristocrats. The memorials and petitions favoring
recharter that daily spilled over the desks of Congressmen he
discounted as the pleas of moneymen, not honest farmers
and workers. Thus when deputations of distinguished citizens
came to Washington to see the President personally and beg
him to restore the deposits, he turned a deaf ear to them.
When they told him they were insolvent, he was contemptuous. "What do you come to me for, then? Go to Nicholas
Biddle. We have no money here, gentlemen. Biddle has all
the money. He has millions of specie in his vaults at this

96. *Ibid.*, 1566.

moment, lying idle, and yet you come to *me* to save you from breaking." [97]

There were other delegations, but to each Jackson insisted he would never recharter the Bank. The panic had been started by Biddle, he said, and if the government capitulated, it would mean that the United States government would be forever subject to the dictates of the monster. It was just a matter of hanging on a little while longer. He had the beast chained, he said. Soon it would be dead.[98]

During these "hundred days," when "men of all sorts, even beardless youths" harangued against him, when a "stream of committees poured upon him," when a "nation seemed to be in arms and the earth in commotion against him," Jackson never appeared "more truly heroic and grand than at this time," reported Thomas Hart Benton. The President "was perfectly mild in his language, cheerful in his temper, firm in his conviction; and confident in his reliance on the power in which he put his trust. I have seen him in a great many situations of peril . . . and always saw him firmly relying upon the success of the right through God and the people, and never saw that confidence more firm and steady than now." [99]

The peril was indeed grave in the winter of 1833–34. And what added to the danger was the persistent rumor that the attack against the Second Bank had been initiated all along by New York politicians in order to shift the financial capital of the country from Chestnut Street to Wall Street. In other words a conspiracy existed to enrich New York at the expense of the entire nation. And who were these villains? Martin Van Buren, of course, and his Regency crew. They were the men who had cooked up the plot in the first place and somehow managed to implicate poor Jackson. Just as Calhoun and Peggy O'Neale had been victimized by these scoundrels, now the entire country was to be swindled in a plot to make Van Buren President

97. Parton, *Jackson,* III, 549–550.
98. Jackson to Andrew Jackson, Jr., February 16, 1834, Jackson, *Correspondence,* V, 249.
99. Benton, *Thirty Years' View,* I, 424.

and Wall Street the money center of the nation.

These rumors, which intensified during the panic months, staggered the Democrats. Several members of the Pennsylvania delegation verged on open revolt against the President when they heard the report; so, too, Southerners who were appalled by the declared intention of the plot. "Other desertions are talked of," reported one man, and for a terrible moment it looked as though Jackson's majority in the House of Representatives was about to break up.[100] "The impression had some how gotten abroad very extensively," admitted Benjamin Butler to Thomas Olcott, "that our New York politicians were in favor of a *Bank to be located at N. Y.,* and it was doing immense evil." [101]

Actually the rumors of the New York conspiracy were as old as the Bank War itself. No sooner had Jackson's first message to Congress been printed in December, 1829 than some had gossiped about a plot hatched by Van Buren.[102] Within months, Henry Clay advised Biddle that he had learned from a "most intelligent citizen of Virginia" that "the plan was laid at Richmond during a visit made to that place by the Secy. of State [Van Buren] last autumn [October, 1829], to make the destruction of the Bank the basis of the next Presidential Election. The message of the President and other indications, are the supposed consequences of that plan." [103]

The friends of Calhoun were another source of the "conspiracy" rumors. They could and did believe anything subversive about Van Buren; after all, if the Magician could displace Calhoun as heir apparent with practically a flick of his finger, nothing could withstand his evil arts.[104] But a lot of the talk about a conspiracy came out of New York itself and was fed directly to Biddle. "All the opposition has been manufactured here," wrote one man in Albany, "here is the central

100. "Recollections of an Old Stager," *Harpers* (1872), XLV, 602.

101. Butler to Olcott, February 1, 1834, Olcott Papers, CUL.

102. Frank O. Gatell, "Sober Second Thoughts on Van Buren, The Albany Regency, and the Wall Street Conspiracy," *Journal of American History* (June, 1966), LIII, 21–21 note 13.

103. Clay to Biddle, June 14, 1830, Biddle Papers, LC.

104. New York *Enquirer,* December 25, 1829.

power." [105] "The head & front of the opposition to the U.S.Bank here are to be found in the Cashier of the Mechanics & Farmers Bank of this city, Mr. Olcott," wrote another.[106] However, a few of Biddle's correspondents nailed Van Buren as the arch foe. "All our attacks on the Bank," said Roswell L. Colt, "come from Van. B." [107]

It was to be expected that the enemies of Van Buren and the Regency would see in the awesome power of the New York politicians and their machine the strength necessary to assault as powerful an institution as the Bank. But no such intrigue ever existed. Although the Regency cronies had economic interests to satisfy they would never propose a third national bank in New York City. If anything they would select Albany. But should they attempt such a scheme they recognized that they would instantly annihilate Van Buren's prospects for the presidency. Pennsylvania, so essential to a national election, would never support him. Nor would the South. Though they might conjecture about the possibility of a new bank and discuss its features, the Regency never considered New York City for a moment. Their letters speak only of the District of Columbia as a possible site.

Biddle knew that the Regency did not initiate the War. Periodically he vented his rage at Van Buren because of the Vice President's influence over Jackson, but he understood that the push and direction of the attack upon the BUS emanated from the White House. James Robertson, the cashier of the Richmond branch of the Bank, declared emphatically to Biddle that, "With regard to the story of a combination between certain politicians and the Secretary of State against the Bank of the U.S., I never did, and do not now believe that there was the slightest foundation for it." As a matter of fact, during Van Buren's trip to Richmond in the fall of 1829, which was supposedly the foundation for the conspiracy theory, no one,

105. S. De Witt Bloodgood to Biddle, September 27, 1833, Biddle Papers, LC.

106. Bloodgood to Biddle, April 18, 1831, Biddle Papers, LC.

107. Colt to Biddle, February 8, 1831, Biddle Papers, LC. See also Charles Davis to Biddle, May 21, 1830, Biddle Papers, LC.

continued Robertson, "heard the name of the Bank, nor an allusion to it, escape his lips." [108]

Yet the fact that no conspiracy existed did not prevent men from believing the gossip nor in repeating it. And during the "Panic session," because it was a time of immense tension, Democrats were highly susceptible to rumors of plots and intrigues. Party desertions surged during the winter, and some doubted that Jackson had the strength to hold the party together. Even the normally cool and placid Van Buren became agitated. Because the Bank question was the only issue that could wreck his presidential ambitions in 1836, and because it was steadily depleting Democratic ranks, he expressed his concern to Jackson. What bothered him particularly was the President's "Protest." He feared it might be misunderstood as a denial of the right of the Congress to provide for the custody, safe-keeping, and disposition of the property and public money of the United States, that Jackson had in effect seized this right for the chief executive. Van Buren urged the General to write a second message and disclaim any such intention. He argued its necessity because their friends were deserting them.

Jackson, very calm and sure of himself, refused to get excited. "Mr. Van Buren," he replied, "*your* friends may be leaving you—but my friends *never* leave *me*." [109]

Even so, the urgency of the request and the wisdom of Van Buren's arguments convinced Jackson to submit a short, four-paragraph message to the Senate on April 21, 1834, which slightly softened the "Protest." He said it was not his intention to deny the right of Congress to provide by law for the disposition of the public money and property, nor to claim for the chief executive the right to dispose of property except under the authority given him by law.[110] Still Jackson knew the value of the original paper and it was that message which was widely published in the newspapers. With the delivery of the second "Protest," the Senate reopened its discussion of executive usur-

108. Robertson to Biddle, November 27, 1830, Biddle Papers, LC.

109. R. H. Wilde to Gulian C. Verplanck, May 1, 1834, Verplanck Papers, NYHS.

110. Richardson, *Messages and Papers,* II, 1312–1313.

pation of power and debated the topic for several more weeks. At the end of the debate the Senate upheld its censure of the President by a vote of 27 to 16.[111]

It was a bad winter. The removal of the deposits, Biddle's squeeze, the economic panic, the rumors of conspiracy, the party desertions, the talk of a new national bank, the political fumbling of the Democrats, the censure of the President, the emergence of the Whig party—all gravely threatened the future of the Jacksonian party. Alarmed and apprehensive, the Democrats groaned their fears, privately and publicly, while the Whigs waited in happy anticipation for the full effects of the President's folly to take hold and reward them with increased political power.

But Jackson fooled them all. Convinced of the rightness of his cause and the ultimate support of the American people, he proceeded to rescue his party and rout the Whigs. Using the vastly strengthened power of the presidency, he closed the Bank War with a stunning display of political skill and ingenuity. And with it he vanquished his enemies: Biddle, the Whigs, the triumvirate—and most especially, the "monster bank."

111. Charles M. Wiltse, *John C. Calhoun, Nullifier* (Indianapolis and New York, 1949), 222.

6

End of the Bank

ESSENTIALLY what Jackson did to close the long War on the Bank was to assert his role as President of the United States and as leader of the Democratic party. The combination exercised by someone as popular as Jackson proved unbeatable. With all the Bank's money, with all the talents of Clay, Webster, and Calhoun backed by a Senate majority, not one or all of them could subdue this pile-driving, popular, democratically aggressive President.

In asserting leadership, Jackson laid down a hard line from which he never deviated. Although at the beginning of the session he was cautious in pushing the line, he became more forceful as the weeks went by and the dangers to his party became more apparent. That line was simple and explicit: he would not recharter the Bank and he would not restore the deposits. Even though he was badgered and begged to soften his stand, he would not yield. To every delegation of Congressmen or businessmen who pleaded with him he replied quietly but "explicitly that the name of Andrew Jackson would never be signed to a bill or resolution to place the Public money in the Bank of the United States or to renew the Charter of that Bank." [1] This did not mean that he would refuse to sanction a third Bank; but it did mean that as far as he was concerned Biddle's corporation was finished. "Were all the worshippers of the golden Calf to memorialise me and request a restoration of the Deposits," he wrote Van Buren, "I would cut my right hand from my body before I would do such an act. The golden

1. C. W. Lawrence to George Newbold, February 9, 1834, Newbold Papers, NYHS.

calf may be worshipped by others but as for myself I will serve the Lord." [2]

One danger in all this, which Jackson certainly understood, was the imputation that he was destroying the Bank in order to replace it with an exact copy, but one colored to his own political persuasion. Because the charge was untrue and because he was committed to a "fair experiment" in deposit banking, Jackson went out of his way to assure the public that he was not involved in a vindictive dog-fight with Biddle personally. His vehicle of communication was the Washington *Globe,* and Blair repeated the President's position in clear and unequivocal terms. "An effort is made, in secret whispers here," reported the *Globe* on February 11, 1834, "to produce an impression that the President . . . is opposed only to *the* Bank of the United States, but not to *a* Bank." The paper added that the President wished it known, and indeed the *Globe* was authorized to state, "that all reports to the contrary are mere inventions of the enemy—*and that the President is firmly resolved to adhere to his plan of the State Banks."*

At least for the moment. And because the moment was so alarming to the Democrats, Jackson was obliged to show a strong and unwavering position with respect to deposit banking. Yet he was enough of a pragmatist and politician to recognize that if the state banks could not do the job he would have to go back to some system of national banking, however distasteful it might be to him.[3] For the moment, however, he was committed to his experiment, and that would go on until it proved a failure. Moreover, he quickly discovered that the deposit system afforded him extraordinary powers in arranging fiscal matters, and Jackson became increasingly reluctant to see them slip back to a central bank.

But more important to the Democratic cause than holding a strong line on the Bank issue was the necessity of close cooperation between the White House and the Jacksonians in Congress to produce a united front against the Bank. This be-

2. Jackson to Van Buren, January 3, 1834, Van Buren Papers, LC.
3. Butler to Olcott, January 27, February 1, March 20, 1834, Olcott Papers, CUL.

came the President's paramount objective all during the "Panic session." To achieve it he initiated close relations with leaders in Congress.[4] For example, the Speaker, Andrew Stevenson, received direction both verbal and written, and since he was an "intimate" of Roger B. Taney he was in almost daily consultation with him throughout the winter months.[5] Polk, chairman of the Ways and Means Committee, was an old friend from Tennessee and a frequent guest at the White House, as was Senator Benton. Both men enjoyed the President's confidence, and if Polk fumbled at the beginning of the session he never lost Jackson's respect for his legislative ability.

Through Stevenson, Polk, Benton, and others, the President repeatedly sought to reach into Congress and control the appointment of important committees. In his *Memoirs,* Hugh Lawson White, Senator from Tennessee, explained Jackson's technique. At an earlier time, shortly before the naming of one important Congressional committee, White, who would be instrumental in its selection, received a note from the President asking him to drop around for a chat. Under the circumstances, White thought it a poor idea and so begged off. A day or so later he met Jackson and the President told him frankly he wanted to keep one man off the committee because he was "hostile to the administration." White thought it a matter *"above party."* Jackson disagreed. Anyway, White said it was too late because he had already submitted the names of the committeemen to the secretary of the Senate before the last adjournment. Jackson then asked him if he could not go back to the secretary that very evening "and substitute some other name" before the Senate Journal was made up. White was shocked, claiming it would be improper to do so. Jackson looked amazed, then abruptly ended the interview.[6]

In other ways Jackson tried to control the activities of Congress, sometimes successfully, sometimes not. One of his less notable attempts was his effort to manipulate the election of

4. Taney to Polk, March 11, 1834, Polk Papers, LC.

5. Taney, "Bank War Manuscript," Taney Papers, LC.

6. Nancy C. Scott, ed., *A Memoir of Hugh Lawson White* (Philadelphia, 1856), 300.

Polk as Speaker of the House. On another occasion, when the Representatives wrangled over a procedural problem concerning the removal, the President pressed the House leaders to stop the debate. Although he failed, he kept a steady flow of information channeled into Congress to buttress Democratic arguments. Also, he ordered his advisers, especially the members of the Kitchen Cabinet, to work intimately with the leadership of both houses. Kendall and Blair were so attentive to their instructions that they were repeatedly accused of improper lobbying in Congress.[7]

Not only did Jackson assert his leadership of the Democratic party in Congress, but he also asserted that leadership around the country. Specifically, he called for mass meetings and legislative caucuses to be held in all the states. Presidential leadership, as far as Jackson practiced it, was based on mass participation, organized by the party, and united behind him for national action. The policy of the opposition, he wrote, was "to cut up the party which had sustained the Administration. . . . Creating divisions among the people as to men, is one of the artifices, essential to the success of the *few* over the *many*. It is therefore of the utmost importance, that the majority should adopt some means to prevent such divisions. The Democratic party of Pennsylvania, and of several other states, have adopted the plan of calling [a] Convention of Delegates, elected by the people themselves and charged with their instructions for the purpose of selecting candidates for important trusts and of thus producing concert among the friends of the same principles. This plan has had the most beneficial operation, in preventing distractions among the people of these states in selecting agents to give effect to their wishes, and in maintaining their control in the Government. It strikes me that this is the only mode by which the people, will be able long to retain in their own hands, the election of President and Vice President." [8]

"Get up meetings and memorials," Jackson told Van Buren,

7. Jackson to Van Buren, January 3, 1834, Van Buren Papers, LC.
8. Jackson to Tilghman A. Howard, August 20, 1833, Jackson, *Correspondence,* V, 166.

and "let the U.S. Bank turn its screws" all it will.[9] Although
not very successful in getting up memorials, state leaders held
many meetings during the "Panic session" to reaffirm their
support of the President. Ohio was one of the first to respond to
the call. Its legislature roundly condemned the Bank and approved the removal. Indiana, Illinois, Tennessee, North Carolina, and Maryland staged Democratic meetings, and these
were especially effective in counteracting the desertion of important Democrats that was still plaguing the party. The Regency, of course, produced some of the grandest meetings in
New York. Instructions went out of Washington early in 1834
"requesting" the state legislature to pass a series of resolutions
against the Bank, that, said Silas Wright, should: "express a
clear, concise, and firm opinion approving of the change of the
deposits"; approve the reasons given by Taney for the removal; oppose the recharter of the present Bank; and approve
the communication read to the Cabinet on September 18. Not
only did the New York legislature perform as "requested," but
city wards and county meetings all across the state passed similar resolutions.[10]

Jackson also encouraged local politicians. At one point he
was asked by a Tennessean for advice about becoming a successful candidate for office. In his reply, Jackson started by referring to the Bank War. It was "a struggle between the people
and aristocracy whether the people shall govern, or whether
they shall be governed of Bank monopolies, and corrupt aristocrats. I tell you if you want to become a conspicuous political
character come out now boldly & fearlessly and my life upon it
you will succeed." Of course, Jackson continued, a politician
must organize his campaign. Therefore, the first thing to do "is
consult your friends," then call a meeting through the newspapers "and get the ball rolling & it will roll over the whole
State in six weeks."[11]   Like any political President, Jackson
tried to control newspapers, at least to the extent of feeding

9. Jackson to Van Buren, January 3, 1834, Van Buren Papers, LC.
10. Wright to Azariah C. Flagg, January 4, 1834, Flagg Papers,
NYPL; Resolutions from the 4th Ward of the Democratic Party, New
York City, January 29, 1834, Van Buren Papers, LC.
11. Jackson to R. M. Barton, May 14, 1835, Jackson Papers, ML.

them acceptable news stories. As a general policy he prodded editors into publishing speeches of Congressmen favorable to the administration. Sometimes these speeches were reprinted in Washington and then mailed directly to newspaper editors under the franking privilege. Senator Hugh Lawson White said that when Jackson got himself worked up into a campaign he "became more and more open and undisguised in his interference to influence and control public opinion. I am well acquainted with his signature," continued White, "and have seen many newspapers and other publications sent under his frank to individuals, and to members of assembly, calculated and intended to injure, in public estimation, those who were unwilling to act in accordance with his wishes. . . ." But those who cooperated with him found he was an extremely valuable supporter, in more ways than one. When Polk, for example, delivered one notable speech in the House in December, 1834, approving removal, Jackson had copies of it distributed "far and wide." [12]

In exercising party leadership, Jackson treated individual Congressmen according to his appraisal of what would produce the fastest results. During the "Panic session" he was deliberately gracious and gentle at one moment, sharp and abrasive the next. With Southerners, generally, he was soothing and pleasant. In view of his recent Nullification fight this was predictable. But with the Pennsylvania delegation, which had led the movement toward desertion from the party, he was merciless. "I am told," reported a Pennsylvania Whig, "that he absolutely rode with whip and spur over our delegation who were so overwhelmed that they had nothing to say for themselves." [13]

When Congressmen cooperated with the President's program, Jackson was all sweetness and Southern charm, frequently inviting them over to the White House for refreshments and his warm thanks. But then they failed him or crossed him, he was no man to encounter. Anyone coming to the White House was warned away by the doorkeeper, who simply informed the

12. Scott, ed., *Memoir of Hugh White,* 301; Sellers, *Polk,* 218.
13. Joseph Hopkinson to Biddle, February 11, 1834, Biddle Papers, LC.

caller that the President was "in a miserable bad humor."[14]

One of Jackson's most successful actions to weaken the opposition and strengthen the Democrats in 1834 was his decision to order an end to the Bank's operation of paying pensions to Revolutionary War veterans. There had been earlier attempts to take over these funds, with the Regency banker, Thomas Olcott, especially active in using his influence to grab some of the money.[15] But none of these efforts were successful. Then, in January, 1834, Jackson ordered his Secretary of War, Lewis Cass, to instruct Biddle to relinquish all the funds, books, and accounts relating to pensions to the War Department's commissioner of pensions. Biddle rejected the order, declaring that the Bank would not be intimidated by such highhanded and unlawful tactics.[16]

Because of Biddle's rejection, the Secretary of War ordered immediate suspension of pension payments. And, as anticipated, veterans let out a howl of protest. Jackson referred Biddle's refusal to Congress, growling in accompaniment that the Bank not only defied the government but inflicted misery on patriotic Americans who had bravely fought for their country and were now repaid with arrogant contempt. In the House, the President's complaint was referred to the Ways and Means Committee which predictably returned a report rebuking the Bank for causing the suspension of pension payments. In the Senate, on the other hand, the majority voted its agreement with the Bank for refusing to obey an improper order.[17]

The Democrats made considerable political capital out of Biddle's defiance. Their newspapers clubbed him for daring to scorn a presidential decree and for refusing to surrender money that did not belong to him. No one could believe, they chorused, that Jackson, The Hero of the War of 1812, would withhold funds from veterans. Only the Czar of Chestnut Street, who had already produced a panic, was capable of such heartless cruelty.[18]

14. Quoted in Sellers, *Polk,* 242.
15. Butler to Olcott, February 1, 1834, Olcott Papers, CUL.
16. Biddle to Joseph Hopkinson, February 21, 1834, Biddle Papers, LC.
17. Catterall, *Second Bank,* 306–307.
18. See Washington *Globe* for January and February, 1834.

So effective was this propaganda that even Webster urged Biddle to relinquish the pension money. The government's argument, the Senator admitted, was weak. No doubt about that. "But, after all, it is a bad subject to dispute about. The pensioners will not believe [that Jackson] is the cause of keeping back their money," and what is worse they will be prey to the President's other contention that the Bank is a dangerous monopoly and must be liquidated.[19] Several other Whigs concurred in Webster's argument, but Biddle shut his ears to their counsel and so advanced the rapid decline of public support the BUS once enjoyed. Without wishing it, Biddle was helping Jackson kill his Bank.

Another cause of trouble for the Democrats during the "Panic session" which the President expertly handled was the so-called New York conspiracy. It was not enough to deny the reports that a plot existed; they had to be repudiated by the New Yorkers themselves. Consequently, Jackson asked Van Buren to request Silas Wright, the Regency's most able lieutenant in Congress, to give a speech in the Senate which would squash the rumors once and for all.[20] Coming from Wright, the repudiation would be recognized as originating with Van Buren.

The Vice President obliged, but because he invariably pursued a subtle approach in his dealings with politicians he only hinted his request to Wright. The Senator, a big, solidly built man with an impassive and ruddy face, did not catch the hints right off, so the Vice President was forced to speak more directly to get his point across. In the end, Van Buren reported, he was "driven by the pressure of the emergency" to call on Wright at his lodgings and "have a talk with him. . . ." At first he was his usual indirect self, mentioning in passing that Wright had been unduly silent in the Senate and had not "realized the anticipations" of his friends. But as the conversation continued, Van Buren zeroed in on his target. "The President," he said, "as well as myself, feels that his real views have not, thus far, been sufficiently developed on the floor of either House of Congress. . . . We are desirous that a fuller and more authori-

19. Webster to Biddle, February 12, 1834, Biddle Papers, LC.
20. Van Buren, *Autobiography*, 729.

tative exposition of them should be made . . . and that you should make it. The presentation of the proceedings of the New York legislature . . . will present a suitable occasion for such exposition, and I come, at his instance, to entreat you to do him that favor. Are you willing to make it, if I inform you of what the President desires to have said?"

"The administration has several friends in the Senate more competent for the task then myself," replied Wright.

"We do not think so," responded Van Buren, "and even if we did, we would for other reasons, prefer that what is said should come from you." [21]

Wright was no fool. He did not need a second go-round to catch the full implication of that last remark. So he ended the conversation by remarking that if Van Buren would write out some of the things the President wanted said he would be glad to incorporate them into his speech.

The next day, with Van Buren seated in the chair of the presiding officer, Wright rose in the Senate and asked for recognition. He began his address by presenting the resolutions recently passed by the New York legislature condemning the Bank and supporting the President. Within ten minutes of the start of the speech, however, its importance was so obvious that several Whig Senators, including Webster, moved closer to him to catch every word. Clay paced nervously around the chamber, stopping off at different places to stare at Wright, listen more intently, or to sample the various snuff-boxes lying around on the tables. Calhoun, meanwhile, stirred restlessly in his seat, sometimes rolling his chair back and forth as though attempting to induce an hypnotic sleep.[22]

"I go against this bank," Wright proclaimed at the very outset, "and against any and every bank to be incorporated by Congress, whether to be located at Philadelphia, or New York, or any where else within the twenty-four independent States which compose this Confederacy upon the broad ground which admits no compromise, that Congress has not the power, by the Constitution, to incorporate such a bank. . . . Still, we are

21. *Ibid.,* 730.
22. John A. Garraty, *Silas Wright* (New York, 1949), 116.

told by the Senator from Massachusetts that things cannot remain as they are; that unless something . . . be done, the pressure, the distress and the agitation will continue." The true
question, he continued, "is understood by the country, and that
it is assuming an attitude toward the bank which the occasion
calls for. . . . The Country, Mr. President, has approved of
the course of the executive in his attempts to relieve us from the
corrupt and corrupting power and influence of a national bank,
and it will sustain him in the experiment now making. . . ." [23]

Among its many virtues, Wright's speech unequivocally repudiated all connection with a plot to enrich New York. It was
such a forthright statement from the Regency that it produced
a sobering effect on Congressmen and eased the tension among
Democrats about the conspiracy. For his part, Van Buren was
extremely pleased with the general impact of the speech. "The
current is now fast setting the other way," he told Theodore
Sedgewick. "The successful effort of Mr. Wright to force out the
true issue has given a right direction of public sentiment.
. . ." [24] Benjamin Butler agreed with Van Buren, but he also
gave credit to Jackson. It was not until "the strong language of
the President & the explicit assertions" of Wright "that the administration were *really* & in *good faith,* desirous to test" the deposit banking system "and that there was no intention to set up
a new Bank for the benefit of New-York, that the democracy of
Pennsylvania rallied in support of the President. For the last
five or six weeks, the public mind in that state, and in the whole
South, has been highly excited, and the opposition to the Bank
has been daily gaining strength." [25]

Shortly after Wright's speech, that is, by the middle of
February 1834, the current started to turn strongly away from
the Bank and in Jackson's favor. The pro-Bank Governor of
Pennsylvania, George Wolf, in his annual message to the state
legislature, publicly damned Biddle for bringing "indiscriminate ruin" upon the community. No sooner was the message

23. *Register of Debates,* 23rd Congress, 1st Session, 399–402.
24. Van Buren to Sedgewick, February 18, 1834, Sedgewick Papers,
MHS.
25. Butler to Olcott, March 20, 1834, Olcott Papers, CUL.

printed than the state's Democratic party issued a strong statement of support for the President, followed soon after by a
resolution passed in the upper house of the Pennsylvania legislature castigating the Bank for its unconscionable actions. Finally, both United States Senators from the state declared
openly that they could no longer defend Biddle or his Bank.
Jackson was so overjoyed by these sudden developments that
he wrote Wolf and extended to him "my sincere thanks for
the exalted and truly patriotic stand you have taken in the
defence of public liberty." [26]

The action of the Pennsylvania Governor was quickly followed by other governors. William L. Marcy, Regency Governor of New York, wrote a particularly strong denunciation of
the Bank in his annual message, and he recommended to the
legislature that they pass a bill issuing $6 million of 5 per cent
state stock to be loaned to the state banks to meet the emergency created by the Bank.[27] Van Buren congratulated Marcy
for having "nailed the flag of New York to the mast on the side
of the great principle that our Government is only Republican
so long as it conforms to, & executes the regularly expressed
will of the people. . . ." [28] Not much later, newspapers from
every part of the country, which had once defended the Bank,
reversed themselves completely and now spoke of Biddle's policy as contemptible and dangerous to the public welfare. Popular response to the sharp change in editorial attitude—if such
can be gauged by reading newspaper editorials—registered overwhelming approval. "The bankites are thunderstruck," noted
Nathaniel Greene, editor of the Boston *Statesman,* "at this up-
rising of the people." [29]

With his own party rallying behind him, with the people
in apparent support, Jackson proceeded cautiously during the
next several months. Having fought the monster for several
years and having divined its battle strategy, he figured that
Biddle, given time, would make the Bank thoroughly repulsive

26. Jackson to Wolf, February, 1834, Jackson Papers, LC.
27. Catterall, *Second Bank,* 341.
28. Van Buren to Marcy, March 31, 1834, Van Buren Papers, LC.
29. Nathaniel Greene to Levi Woodbury, March 14, 1834, Levi
Woodbury Papers, LC.

to every fair-minded member of Congress. So he waited. Meanwhile, he was gratified to see the Whigs stumbling over themselves because of their own leadership failure in Congress. The coalition of Clay, Webster, and Calhoun was strong as long as it pummeled Jackson for his aggressive use of presidential power. But once it moved beyond that vocal exercise to consider the Bank's recharter, the triumvirate fell apart. Specifically, the three men could not agree on terms. Webster, in an attempt at compromise, proposed chartering the Bank for either three, four or six years beyond 1836, a compromise Biddle was willing to accept. But Clay, resolute against granting any concession to the President, would not hear of compromise. It was to be another twenty-year charter or nothing. So it was nothing, and Webster's plan died aborning. At the same time, Calhoun argued in favor of a system that would convert the United States to the gold standard exclusively. These differences of opinion fissured Whig leadership in Congress; they also tipped off the more perceptive among the party's rank and file that the great triumvirate was less interested in solving the banking problem than in advancing their presidential prospects in 1836. In short, the Bank issue was running out of steam.

As the Whigs faltered in the Senate, the Democrats came alive in the House. After several mishaps they finally broke the debate that held up Taney's report and passed the previous question by a scant four votes. With the report now safely tucked inside Polk's committee, Democrats breathed more easily. In his enthusiasm the chairman even invited Taney to draft the committee's findings to the House, but the Secretary wisely declined. However, both men conferred right up to the final moment of writing the report,[30] and as a consequence that report was a model of partisan polemics. It not only faulted Biddle for starting the panic; it also argued strongly for Jackson's hard-money policy.

Quickened by their new sense of strength and conscious that the current of popular opinion was becoming strongly anti-Bank, the Democratic leaders in Congress rushed a series

30. Sellers, *Polk,* 219.

of resolutions through the House of Representatives that was designed to take full advantage of the moment and permanently block the rechartering of the Bank. The resolutions were steered through Polk's Ways and Means Committee and adopted by the full House on April 4, 1834. There were four. First, by a vote of 134 to 82, the House declared that the Second Bank "ought not to be rechartered"; then, by a vote of 118 to 103, it agreed that the deposits "ought not to be restored"; next, by a vote of 117 to 105, it counseled that the state banks be continued as the places of deposit; and finally, by the overwhelming vote of 175 to 42, the House authorized the selection of a committee to examine the Bank's affairs and investigate the reasons for the panic.[31]

These votes spelled the doom of the Bank. It was now just a matter of time for the Democrats to complete an investigation to prove that Biddle had wantonly and irresponsibly brought economic havoc to the country in order to get his charter. Considering the heated partisanship during the entire War there could be little doubt about the substance of the committee's eventual findings even before the investigation began. But what was significant about the overwhelming approval of the fourth resolution was the apparent conviction on the part of most Congressmen that Biddle had indeed unleashed an economic maelstrom.

Jackson glowed. "I have obtained a glorious triumph," he enthused. "The overthrow of the opposition in the House of Representatives by the vote on the reso[lu]tions . . . was a triumphant one, and put to death, that mamouth of corruption and power, the Bank of the United States."[32] The Attorney General concurred in this judgment of death, but at the same time implied that another national bank was still possible. "The Bank is dead," he told the Regency, ". . . I mean in its present form."[33]

By early spring even the panic eased somewhat, as though

31. *Register of Debates,* 23rd Congress, 1st Session, 3474–3477.
32. Jackson to John Coffee, April 6, 1834, Jackson to Andrew Jackson, Jr., April 6, 1834, Jackson, *Correspondence,* V, 260, 259.
33. Butler to Olcott, June 19, 1834, Olcott Papers, CUL.

responding to the political breakthrough. Biddle, pressured by businessmen and criticized by his staunchest supporters, now slowly loosened his financial grip. It was a gradual loosening, however, and contraction continued until July 1834 when the Bank's board of directors voted unanimously to end all curtailments. Nevertheless, with the passage of each month during the spring, a real change could be felt in all the leading cities. "The clamour of pressure in the money market is vanishing with the panic," wrote Jackson on March 15, "all things will end well here." [34]

Perhaps the last and worst blow the great Bank sustained was struck by Biddle himself. When confronted by the House committee sent out under the fourth resolution to investigate his management, he radiated contempt. Truculent as ever, he refused the committee members permission to examine the Bank's books or the correspondence with Congressmen relating to personal loans from the Bank; also, he refused to testify before the committee. Furious, the investigators returned to Washington and pressed for a citation of contempt. Taney supported this action as did several members of the Kitchen Cabinet, but many House Democrats refused to cooperate with them. As Biddle shrewdly observed, it would be ironic if he went to prison "by the votes of members of Congress because I would not give up to their enemies their confidential letters." [35] Although Biddle escaped punishment by Congress his continued defiance of the government and his obvious attitude that he and his Bank stood above the law only condemned him in the eyes of the public. His latest action, said William Rives, proved "to the people never again to give themselves such a master." [36]

In a desperate effort to ward off the inevitable Biddle asked the friendly Senate to conduct an investigation of the Bank's affairs. On the last day of the session his request was approved and the task referred to the Finance Committee. The

34. Jackson to Samuel Swartwout, March 15, 1834, Jackson Papers, LC.

35. Biddle to J. G. Watmouth, May 2, May 10, 1834, Biddle Papers, LC.

36. Rives to Woodbury, May 26, 1834, Woodbury Papers, LC.

following December, the committee's report, written by John
Tyler of Virginia, was submitted to the Senate. On every important point the committee's findings approved the Bank's
policy and operation. But it was now too late. The report was
submitted after the fall Congressional elections, and since the
people had long since abandoned Biddle and his Bank the
elections produced a phenomenal swelling of popular support
for the Jackson party. Not only did the Democrats increase
their strength in the House but they became the majority party
in the Senate. Whatever faint hope existed for the Bank slowly
faded away.

The verdict now irrevocable, the President declared that the
government would cease accepting branch drafts in the payment of taxes. In addition, to prove the Bank unnecessary, he
promised to give the country a "sound and portable currency." [37] These pronouncements were nails in the Bank's coffin.
Still Biddle refused to lie still. As the new session of Congress
opened, Biddle continued to talk about eventual recharter.
Everyone else knew better. Whigs were deserting the Bank
almost en masse, for they recognized that the issue of recharter
was a political kiss of death. Thurlow Weed, the Whig party
boss in New York, said that for a candidate connected with the
Bank, "the game is up." It would be "*suicidal*" to "carry politics
into business. The poor were almost all against before, and this
course will make them unanimously so. My feeling, and judgment say, make war against the Banks." [38]

In mortally wounding the Bank, President Jackson awarded
himself tremendous powers over the financial operations of the
country. Through his Treasury Secretary, he could direct the
movement of vast sums of money in and out of state banks.
Jackson never intended to seize this power, but the fact remained that he had it. And once taken he was extremely
reluctant to part with it; which is probably one reason why he
continued the experiment of deposit banking long after he knew

37. Richardson, *Messages and Papers,* II, 1329–1331.
38. Weed to Francis Granger, November 23, 1834, Granger Papers,
LC.

it did not work as intended. Simply stated, he enjoyed the exercise of financial control provided by the system. "The presidential power," sighed one Senator, "swallows up all power. . . ." [39]

But another and perhaps more important reason why he continued the experiment was his hope that it would provide a regulated, responsible banking system. To help speed this along Jackson proposed a series of measures in April, 1834 to institute a general reform of currency and banking. It was contained in a report submitted by Taney to the House Ways and Means Committee requesting the following: that the selection of the pet banks be left to the Secretary of the Treasury; that he be permitted to remove the deposits from any bank after submitting his reasons to Congress; that banks submit monthly reports of their condition; that the government have the right to examine the books and records of the pets; that gold be revalued to bring it to a parity with silver; and that the deposit banks be required to cease issuing notes under five dollars. Later the prohibition against paper would be extended to all notes under twenty dollars. In this way the country would be restored to specie for its regular transactions and bank notes would only serve commercial purposes.

This proposal represented a total triumph of Jackson's monetary views. But there was more involved. The obvious strengthening of the President's control over finance through the regulation of a small group of banks alarmed many Congressmen already fearful for the constitutional balance of the three branches of government. The effort to reform the currency, therefore, became entangled in a larger issue, and for the next two years the administration wrestled with Congress to resolve the impasse. Finally, in June 1836, the Deposit Act was enacted which offered a compromise of sorts, but it fell a long distance from Taney's original proposals. It became law over strong administration protests. "With a repugnance of feeling and a recoil of judgment," reported Senator Benton, Jackson

39. John Tyler to Dr. Henry Curtis, March 28, 1834, Tyler, *Letters and Times of the Tylers*, I, 491.

signed the bill only because he believed it would enhance Van
Buren's chances of election to the presidency in 1836.[40]

According to the provisions of the Deposit Act, the Treasury Department's discretion in the selection of the pets was
sharply curtailed. A deposit bank had to be located in each
state, provided certain prescribed conditions were fulfilled. No
transfer of deposits from bank to bank was permissible unless
required by the needs of the Treasury, and, in that case, the
transfer had to go to the nearest bank, not from one end of the
country to the other. The act also limited the amount of federal
money to be held by each bank by stipulating that no pet
could hold government funds in excess of a sum equal to three-
fourths of its capital stock actually paid in. As a result of this
provision the number of deposit banks had to be increased
immediately, and their number soon rose from twenty to
ninety. This increase in the number of pets made it virtually
impossible to exercise any control over them. Indeed, the Deposit Act was extremely vague about regulation of these banks,
which obviously delighted entrepreneurs who soon discovered
that without restrictive controls they could engineer bigger and
more profitable financial deals. The cash and credit were there
practically for the asking.

The Deposit Act also required the pets to redeem all their
notes in specie and to issue no notes for less than five dollars
after July 4, 1836, nor receive any under five dollars in payment
of an obligation owed to the United States. Later the amount
would be raised to ten dollars and by March 3, 1837, to twenty
dollars. The act also stipulated that whenever the amount of
deposit in any bank exceeded one-fourth of the capital stock of
the bank, the pet was required to pay the United States an
interest of two per cent on the excess.

What added considerable attraction to the Deposit Act for
some were its provisions for the distribution of excess federal
money to the states. These provisions were necessitated by the
enormous federal surplus that had been piling up each year.
The surplus resulted from four things: the lack of a national

40. Benton, *Thirty Years' View*, I, 657–8; Gatell, "Spoils of the Bank
War," *American Historical Review*, LXX, 36.

debt, the tariff revenues, land sale revenues, and the general prosperity of the nation. The question which faced Congress was what to do with the surplus. Those anxious to get their hands on it pleaded that it be pumped into the states, but Jackson warned that such action would launch a dangerous inflation. Congress, responsive to the pleas of the nation's entrepreneurs, finally settled the problem by distributing the surplus among the states. This action, which was part of the Deposit Act, stated that all money in the Treasury as of January 1, 1837, in excess of $5 million would be deposited with the several states in proportion to their respective representation in the House and Senate. The money would be distributed in four installments: in January, April, July, and October 1837. The states in return would give the Secretary of the Treasury negotiable certificates of deposits which the Secretary would sell if necessary. These certificates, if negotiated, would bear an interest rate of five per cent.[41]

So what might have been a well regulated banking system consisting of a small group of banks under reasonable federal control and selected for their soundness and ability to influence other banks now became an unregulated collection of nearly a hundred banks with more money than they could properly handle. Jackson clearly disliked both the deposit and distribution features of the law. But what could he do? He had asked for the necessary authority to handle the fiscal problems and had been refused. One possible alternative was another national bank, but Jackson was reluctant at this late date to abandon the deposit system. In part, he was a victim of his own propaganda; in part, he was too stubborn to admit the merits of national banking; in part, he was surrounded by too many men like Kendall and Blair who were committed to the pets; and, in part, he feared jeopardizing his chosen successor's election to the presidency.[42] Besides, what would the people think? They

41. *Niles Weekly Register,* June 25, 1836.
42. Blair's editorials in the *Globe* insisted the President was *"firmly resolved"* to adhere to the pets and have nothing to do with a national bank. These editorials run fairly consistently from the spring of 1834 to the fall of 1836. See also John A. Dix to Azariah C. Flagg, August 20, 1836, Flagg Papers, NYPL.

could easily say he had reversed himself and was now admitting that he had been wrong all along.

Jackson's stubbornness about the value of central banking was a real impediment to the solution of the money problem. In a letter written to Levi Woodbury, the new Secretary of the Treasury, who was appointed after Taney's rejection by the Senate, Jackson urged him to circulate as much gold coin as possible "to convince the people how ideal [sic] & falacious has been all the noise made by the bank men of the necessity of a national Bank to regulate the currency and being necessary as a fiscal agent of the government." [43] The circulation of gold was stimulated somewhat in 1834 when Congress revalued the metal in relation to silver from 15 to 1 to 16 to 1, but it failed to produce the effect the President desired. Also, Woodbury, on his own authority, issued an order prohibiting notes under five dollars, but again this action came too late to check the fast spreading speculative boom that had been generated in large measure by the deposit system. State banks, without any real control over their operations and backed by government funds to the tune of $22.35 million,[44] inundated the country with their paper. Soon there were hundreds of different kinds of paper in circulation, some of it from places with such harrowing names as "Glory Bank." The very thing the President had sought to prevent was now running out of control.

If there had been any doubts in Jackson's mind about the failure of his "experiment," they vanished now. Discouraged, he pondered possible alternatives still open to him. He told Amos Kendall in 1836 he was considering the establishment of a Bank of Deposit and Exchange in Washington, one that would report annually to Congress "its whole proceedings, with the name of all debtors &c &c." This bank would also have the power to issue bills over twenty dollars. Jackson thought such a project might be a good example for the states as well as prove beneficial to the "safety of our currency . . . check the paper system & gambling menace that pervades our land & must

43. Jackson to Woodbury, July 3, 1834, Woodbury Papers, LC.

44. The 22.35 million is the amount at the end of 1835. Scheiber, "Pet Banks in Jacksonian Politics and Finance, 1833–1841," *Journal of Economic History* (June, 1963), XXIII, 202.

if not checked ruin our country & our liberty." [45] But it was too late now to make changes. His administration was nearly over. Besides, this was a presidential election year, and Jackson would never hazard his party by proposing a new bank. Politics stayed his hand, despite his agonized fears over the inflation.

As the speculative boom worsened, commanding presidential action, Jackson tried to halt it and strengthen his hard-money policy by ordering the government's land offices, where much of the country's speculative mania was centered, to refuse paper money under five dollars in the payment of public lands. Finally, in July 1836, Jackson went beyond this initial directive and decreed that henceforth only gold and silver was acceptable for the purchase of public lands. This Specie Circular, a well-intentioned and forceful exercise of executive authority, brought a jarring halt to the speculative drive, but no amount of last-minute presidential action could shield the nation against a full-blown depression which swept the entire country less than a year later.[46]

Among his several faults and mistakes, Jackson was naive about the advantages of hard money—and a little foolish too. He was fortunate to be President at a time when the country was experiencing great economic growth that required concomitant expansions of credit and currency. By his actions in killing the Bank and providing state banks with government funds he unintentionally made available the mightiest ingredients of industrial growth and development. The government's money not only supported speculation but advanced the full implementation of the industrial revolution.

As for the United States Bank, it died a slow demeaning death. Remaining popular support rapidly drained away because of the panic and because of Biddle's refusal to surrender the pension money or submit to a Congressional investigation. With each election the people reaffirmed their desire to have

45. Jackson to Kendall, November 24, 1836, Jackson-Kendall Papers, LC. See also Jackson to Woodbury, July 3, 8, August 15, 1834, Woodbury Papers, LC.
46. Richard H. Timberlake, Jr., "The Specie Circular and Distribution of the Surplus," *The Journal of Political Economy* (April, 1960), LXVIII, 117.

done with the monster, until even the Senate held a majority of Democrats. Now there was nothing left for the bank to do but close up shop. Indeed, when Jackson declared that branch drafts were no longer acceptable for the payment of government taxes, Biddle began preparing for the final closing although he continued to talk about possible recharter. Branches were sold, and the proceeds from the sale of bills of exchange were transmitted to Philadelphia. "The bank," Biddle wrote in August, 1835, "is winding up its affairs, quietly and certainly. . . . Our great object is to close its concerns in such a manner as to avoid all pressure." [47]

Nothing was left the unfortunate Bank. Even the censure of the President for his actions against the BUS was expunged by the Senate once the Democrats gained control of Congress. On January 16, 1837, by the vote of 24 to 19, the upper house agreed to erase the stricture from its Journal. Immediately after the vote Senator Benton moved that the secretary of the Senate, Asbury Dickens, proceed to carry out the order. As Asbury took the appropriate Journal from the shelf and prepared to execute the order, most of the Whigs walked out of the chamber to demonstrate their disapproval. Then the gallery set up a commotion and began hissing the action of the clerk. Benton, enraged by the discourtesy, sprang to his feet.

"Bank ruffians! Bank ruffians!" he cried. "Seize them, sergeant-at-arms! Here is one," he shouted, "just above me, that may easily be identified—the bank ruffian."

When order was restored the clerk returned to his task. He carefully drew broad black lines around the resolution passed in 1834 and across its face wrote: "Expunged by order of the Senate, this 16th day of January, 1837." [48]

With the end of the Bank, now that its charter had expired, Biddle sought to keep the Philadelphia branch in operation by applying for incorporation in Pennsylvania. Although some Democrats opposed the move on principal, the state legislature issued a charter to the bank in 1836. But it was dearly bought, costing nearly $6 million. Biddle felt he had no choice but to

47. Biddle to Silas M. Sitwell, August 24, 1835, Biddle Papers, LC.
48. Poore, *Reminiscences,* 142; Wise, *Seven Decades,* 143.

pay the fee; still it was a very heavy burden to carry, particularly with a depression looming on the horizon. To add to its problems, the bank borrowed heavily in Europe, another burden to freight during the panic; and it engineered a wild scheme to corner the cotton market and support the price of cotton in a falling market. When the cotton prices continued to slide the bank was forced to draw more and more on its credit, until at last that credit vanished. Resorting to questionable operations on Wall Street to maintain solvency, the bank squandered its prestige and reputation. Soon smart investors sold its stock. With credit and reputation gone, the bank closed its doors in 1841, dragging down a number of other banks across the country.[49]

Biddle resigned as president in March 1839, but he was responsible for the cotton speculation that ended so disastrously. He was sued for nearly a quarter of a million dollars by irate stockholders, who, earlier, had given him a magnificent service of gold plate upon his retirement. Later he was arrested on charges of criminal conspiracy, or, in the words of Philip Hone, for "high crimes and vulgar misdemeanors by a secret conclave of greasy householders. . . ."[50] The court, however, freed him. Other litigations followed but they terminated abruptly when Biddle died on February 27, 1844, at the age of 58, of bronchitis complicated by dropsy.

Even in death the Democrats gave him no peace. They jeered him as he was lowered into his grave. William Cullen Bryant, the Jacksonian editor and poet, noted that Biddle had "died at his country-seat, where he passed the last of his days in elegant retirement, which, if justice had taken place, would have been spent in the penitentiary."[51]

49. Smith, *Economic Aspects,* 200–201, 219–220, 226–227.
50. Philip Hone, *The Diary of Philip Hone* (New York, 1889), II, 104.
51. *Ibid.,* 206.

7

In Retrospect

THE BANK OF THE UNITED STATES died ignominiously—and needlessly. It got caught in a death struggle between two willful, proud, stubborn men. Jackson and Biddle were both responsible for permitting what could have been prevented. Both were reckless, both insufferably arrogant and vindictive. Between them they crushed a useful institution that had provided the country with sound currency and ample credit. At any number of points during the long controversy they could have compromised their differences and allowed the Bank to continue to serve the nation. Instead they preferred to sacrifice it to their need for total victory.

In the hindsight that history provides, there is no question that the Second Bank of the United States needed curbing. It concentrated too much power in private hands, power that was repeatedly misused. In the hands of someone as capable as Nicholas Biddle, who could run financial rings around any and all of the Secretaries of the Treasury he faced, that power had to be carefully circumscribed. Granted Jackson provoked the Bank; the fact remains that it could inflict economic havoc at will, subvert the intentions of the administration, and defy the orders of the government. Thus it had to be reformed. But if curbing was impossible, as events subsequently proved, then, regrettably, it merited killing.

In abolishing one efficient central banking system, Jackson can be faulted for not substituting another: one better controlled but one able to provide the country with adequate currency and credit. Some historians feel that his failure here condemned the nation to a century of unsound finance, and also, that after the Civil War, it encouraged robber barons to take advantage of their freedom and systematically pillage the country. However, in view of the failure of a later central bank, the Federal Reserve System, to control economic opportunists in the 1920's, this criticism seems overly severe.

But more important than the economic effects of the Bank War was its significance in party development, and particularly in the growth of presidential power. It is clear that in terms of party history the Bank War was the single most important event during the entire middle period of American history. Not only did it give rise to the Whig party, but the clash between the opposing Bank forces established rigid lines between the contending parties that lasted practically to the Civil War. It exalted such things as party loyalty; it demonstrated that the President could be a politician of the masses; and it fashioned the character of the Democratic party in terms of leadership, organizational discipline, and popular following for nearly a generation.

Even more significant, the Bank War became the instrument by which the powers of the President were vastly expanded. Whether justified or not, Jackson succeeded in destroying a powerful institution deeply entrenched in the economic (if not political) life of the country. To do this, he enlarged the authority of the chief executive in several ways: He stretched the veto power and claimed the right to block legislation for reasons of policy or expediency rather than constitutionality. Thereafter, Congress carefully considered the presidential will in *all* legislation in order to avoid a possible veto. Next, he broadened the political power base of the presidency by taking the Bank issue to the people and winning an overwhelming victory in the presidential election of 1832. Thereafter Jackson did not hesitate to claim an augmentation of executive authority by virtue of this victory at the polls. More important, he *demonstrated* this authority by destroying the Bank over intense Congressional opposition. In addition, Jackson widened the President's responsibility to include all the people, a necessary acknowledgment if he was to draw political strength from their support when he tangled with Congress. Moreover, he advanced the concept that the President is the direct (and sole) representative of the people, a revolutionary concept for its time. Lastly, he settled the question that the President has absolute power to remove subordinate executive officers at will.

In the course of the Bank War, Jackson used the presidency for purposes of national leadership. In the process he narrowed the distance between the President and Congress and between the President and the electorate. By his constant appeal for popular support in the important issues facing his administration, Jackson encouraged democratic attitudes among the people. To a large extent he presumed mass participation in the government via the presidential office.

Today, the system of American government requires strong executive action to accomplish the purposes of democracy. Since the office did not come equipped with the necessary powers under the original Constitution, they had to be added through an historical process by the aggressive action of vigorous Presidents. Andrew Jackson was one of a half dozen Presidents who rapidly advanced the role of the executive within the federal government. In his two terms in office he virtually remade the presidency; and he did it, to a large extent, during the Bank War.

A Bibliographical Review

THE LITERATURE OF the Jacksonian era is quite extensive, as anyone who has tried to keep a check on it can readily attest. Fortunately, there are several historiographical guides to assist the reader in finding his way through it, the most useful being Alfred A. Cave, *Jacksonian Democracy and the Historians* (Gainesville, Florida, 1964). Charles G. Sellers, Jr. has two articles which carefully analyze the direction Jacksonian scholarship has pursued in the last century or more: "Andrew Jackson versus the Historians," *Mississippi Valley Historical Review* (March, 1958), XLIV, 615–634, and *Jacksonian Democracy,* Publication No. 9, Service Center for Teachers of History (Washington, 1958). Also helpful is the chapter entitled, "The Age of the Common Man," by John William Ward in John Higham, ed., *The Reconstruction of American History* (New York, 1962).

On the Bank War itself, the most satisfactory work is still Ralph C. H. Catterall, *The Second Bank of the United States* (Chicago, 1903), although it does not carry the story through the final years of the Bank's history after the charter had expired. Bray Hammond's *Bank and Politics in America from the Revolution to the Civil War* (Princeton, 1957) is a monumental work deserving every praise and prize it has won. It is particularly valuable in identifying the entrepreneurial thrust of the Jacksonians in waging their war against the Bank. But Hammond seriously underestimates the role played by Jackson in the War and overstates the role of men like Van Buren, Taney, Hill, Blair, Kendall, Cambreleng, and others. The result constitutes an unintended but serious misrepresentation of Jacksonian politics. As I see it, the Bank War was essentially a political struggle, with the President calling the shots, and only secondarily an economic battle among various "men on the make." Another work which denies Jackson's central role in this era is Lee Benson's *The Concept of Jacksonian Democracy: New York as a Test Case* (Princeton, 1961), a book otherwise notable for its unusual methodological approach to the documentary evidence of this period. There is a valuable chapter on Jackson in Richard Hofstadter's *The American*

Political Tradition and the Men Who Made It (New York, 1948);
and Glyndon G. Van Deusen's *The Jacksonian Era, 1828–1848*
(New York, 1959) is useful as a general survey of the entire age.

A work of scholarly precision and detail, though highly prejudiced in favor of its subject, is Thomas Govan's biography of
Nicholas Biddle (Chicago, 1959). Despite the prejudice, it is a
sound book, correct in almost every important aspect of the War.
Also valuable in understanding the economic problems involved in
destroying the Bank are Fritz Redlich, *The Moulding of American
Banking: Men and Ideas,* Part I (New York, 1947), Sister M. Grace
Madeleine, *Monetary and Banking Theories of Jacksonian Democ-
racy* (Philadelphia, 1943), and Walter Buckingham Smith, *Economic
Aspects of the Second Bank of the United States* (Cambridge, 1953).

There are several biographies of the leading figures in the controversy. James Parton's *Life of Andrew Jackson* (3 vols., New
York, 1961) contains many first hand accounts of various aspects
of the struggle. Useful for color and dramatic highlight is Marquis
James' *The Life of Andrew Jackson* (two vols. in one, Indianapolis
and New York, 1938); but more critical and scholarly is John S.
Bassett, *The Life of Andrew Jackson* (two vols. in one, New York,
1928). A short one-volume study is Robert V. Remini's *Andrew
Jackson* (New York, 1966), while William Graham Sumner's *Andrew Jackson* (Boston and New York, 1882) offers a detailed narrative of the War.

Biographies of Jackson's contemporaries who influenced the
struggle constitute something of a mixed bag. Regrettably, there
are no biographies of Martin Van Buren, Amos Kendall, Isaac Hill,
or Frank P. Blair, although Blair is accounted for to some extent
in William E. Smith's *The Francis Preston Blair Family In Politics*
(2 vols., New York, 1933), and Van Buren in Edward M. Shep-
ard's study (Boston, 1899). There are two able biographies of Benton: Elbert B. Smith's *Magnificent Missourian: The Life of Thomas
Hart Benton* (Philadephia, 1958) and William N. Chambers, *Old
Bullion Benton, Senator From the New West* (Boston, 1956); and
two on Taney, one by Carl Swisher, *Roger B. Taney* (New York,
1936) and one by Walker Lewis, *Without Fear or Favor: A Biography of Chief Justice Roger Brooke Taney* (New York, 1965).
Two books of tremendous value, but for different reasons, are:
Charles G. Sellers, Jr., *James K. Polk, Jacksonian, 1795–1843*
(Princeton, 1957) and Charles Wiltse, *John C. Calhoun, Nullifier*
(Indianapolis and New York, 1949). Other useful biographies include: Glyndon G. Van Deusen, *The Life of Henry Clay* (Boston,
1937); Clement Eaton, *Henry Clay and the Art of American Politics* (Boston, 1957); Samuel Flagg Bemis, *John Quincy Adams and
the Union* (New York, 1955); Claude M. Fuess, *Daniel Webster*

(2 vols., Boston, 1930); Richard N. Current, *Daniel Webster and the Rise of National Conservatism* (Boston, 1955); Philip S. Klein, *President James Buchanan* (University Park, Pa., 1962); Eugene I. McCormac, *James K. Polk* (Berkeley, 1922); Robert Seager, *And Tyler Too* (New York, 1963); Joseph H. Parks, *Felix Grundy* (Baton Rouge, 1940); John A. Garraty, *Silas Wright* (New York, 1949); Ivor D. Spencer, *The Victor and the Spoils: A Life of William L. Marcy* (Providence, Rhode Island, 1959); and Gerald Capers, *John C. Calhoun: Opportunist* (Gainesville, 1962).

Worthy of attention are a number of excellent books dealing with aspects of banking or banking theory, both state and national. These include: Richard H. Timberlake, *Money, Banking, and Central Banking* (New York, 1965); Davis R. Dewey, *State Banking Before the Civil War* (Washington, 1910); H. E. Miller, *Banking Theories in the United States Before 1860* (Cambridge, 1927); J. Ray Cable, *The Bank of the State of Missouri* (New York, 1923); Stephen A. Caldwell, *A Banking History of Louisiana* (Baton Rouge, 1935); Claude A. Campbell, *The Development of Banking in Tennessee* (Nashville, 1932); Robert E. Chaddock, *The Safety Fund Banking System in New York, 1829–1866* (Washington, 1910); Matthew S. Clarke, *Legislative and Documentary History of the Bank of the United States* (Washington, 1832); George W. Dowrie, *The Development of Banking in Illinois* (Urbana, Illinois, 1913); General Basil Duke, *History of the Bank of Kentucky* (Louisville, 1895); William M. Gouge, *Journal of Banking* (Philadelphia, 1842) and *Short History of Paper Money and Banking* (New York, 1835); Joseph Hedges, *Commercial Banking and the Stock Market Before 1863* (Baltimore, 1938); Leonard C. Helderman, *National and State Banks* (Boston and New York, 1931); Ralph Hidy, *The House of Baring in American Trade and Finance* (Cambridge, 1949); John Thom Holdsworth, *The First and Second Banks of the United States* (Washington, 1910); Charles C. Huntington, *A History of Banking and Currency in Ohio Before the Civil War* (Columbus, 1915); John J. Knox, *History of Banking in the United States* (New York, 1900); Josiah G. Leach, *The History of the Girard National Bank of Philadelphia, 1832–1902* (Philadelphia, 1902); Lloyd W. Mints, *A History of Banking Theory* (Chicago, 1945); Francis Parsons, *A History of Banking in Connecticut* (New Haven, 1935); John G. Ranlett, *Money and Banking* (New York, 1965); William L. Royall, *Andrew Jackson and the Bank of the United States* (New York, 1880); William Graham Sumner, *History of Banking in the United States* (New York, 1896); and Esther Taus, *Central Banking Functions of the United States Treasury* (New York, 1943).

Scholarly articles appearing in various learned journals were particularly important in the preparation of this monograph. Frank

Otto Gatell has written three significant articles: "Spoils of the Bank War: Political Bias in the Selection of Pet Banks," *American Historical Review* (October, 1964), LXX, 35–58; "Sober Second Thoughts on Van Buren, The Albany Regency, and the Wall Street Conspiracy," *The Journal of American History* (June, 1966), LIII, 19–40; and "Secretary Taney and the Baltimore Pets: A Study in Banking and Politics, *Business History Review* (Summer, 1965), XXXIX, 205–227. A paper Gatell read at the 1966 meeting of the American Historical Association in New York City, entitled "Money and Party in Jacksonian America: A Quantitative Look at New York's Men of Quality" successfully refutes the thesis that the leadership of both the Democratic and Whig parties in New York came from the same socioeconomic strata. This paper will be published in the June 1967 issue of the *Political Science Quarterly*. An extremely valuable article on the background of Jackson's banking views is Charles G. Sellers, Jr., "Banking and Politics in Jackson's Tennessee, 1817–1827," *Mississippi Valley Historical Review* (June, 1954), XLI, 61–84.

Other notable articles include: Richard H. Timberlake, Jr, "The Specie Circular and Distribution of Surplus," *The Journal of Political Economy* (April, 1960), LXVIII, 109–117; Harry N. Scheiber, "The Pet Banks in Jacksonian Politics and Finance, 1833–1841," *Journal of Economic History* (June, 1963), XXIII, 196–214; Lynn Marshall, "The Authorship of Jackson's Bank Veto Message," *Mississippi Valley Historical Review* (December, 1963), L, 466–477; Jacob Meerman, "The Climax of the Bank War: Biddle's Contraction, 1833–34," *The Journal of Political Economy* (August, 1963), LXXI, 378–388; and Leon Schur, "Second Bank of the United States and the Inflation After the War of 1812," *The Journal of Political Economy* (April, 1960), LXVIII, 118–134.

Three articles by Bray Hammond are helpful, although much of the material was later incorporated into his *Banks and Politics*. They include: "Jackson, Biddle, and the Bank of the United States," *The Journal of Economic History* (May, 1947), VII, 1–23, "Banking in the Early West: Monopoly, Prohibition and Laissez Faire," *The Journal of Economic History* (May, 1948), VIII, 1–25; and "Public Policy and National Banks," which is a review of Arthur M. Schlesinger, Jr., *The Age of Jackson* in *The Journal of Economic History* (May, 1946), VI, 79–84. Other useful or significant scholarly articles, include: Thomas P. Abernethy, "The Early Development of Commerce and Banking in Tennessee," *Mississippi Valley Historical Review* (December, 1927), XIV, 311–325; Hattie M. Anderson, "Frontier Economic Problems in Missouri, 1815–1828," *Missouri Historical Review* (October, 1939), XXXIV, 38–70; Kenneth L. Brown, "Stephen Girard, Promoter of the Second Bank of the United

States," *Journal of Economic History* (1942), II, 125–148; J. Ray Cable, "Some Early Missouri Bankers," *Missouri Historical Review* (January, 1932), XXVI, 117–119; Guy S. Callender, "The Early Transportation and Banking Enterprises of the States in Relation to the Growth of Corporations," *Quarterly Journal of Economics* (November, 1902), XVII, 111–162; Harold E. Davis, "Economic Basis of Ohio Politics, 1820–40," *Ohio Archaeological and Historical Quarterly* (October, 1938), XLVII, 290–309; Logan Esarey, "The First Indiana Banks," *Indiana Quarterly Magazine of History* (December, 1910), VI, 144–158; Thomas P. Govan, "Banking and the Credit System in Georgia, 1816–60," *Journal of Southern History* (May, 1938), IV, 164–184; Elmer C. Griffith, "Early Banking in Kentucky," *Proceedings of the Mississippi Valley Historical Association* (1908–9), II, 168–181; Samuel Reyneck, "Social History of an American Depression, 1837–1843," *American Historical Review* (July, 1935), XL, 662–687, and "The Depression of 1819–22, A Social History," *American Historical Review* (October, 1933), XXXIX 28–47; John J. Rowe, "Money and Banks in Cincinnati Before the Civil War," *Bulletin of the Historical and Philosophical Society of Ohio* (July 1948), VI, 74–84; O.M.W. Sprague, "Branch Banking in the United States," *Quarterly Journal of Economics* (1902–3), XVII, 242–260; Glyndon G. Van Deusen, "Some Aspects of Whig Thought and Theory in the Jacksonian Period," *American Historical Review* (January, 1959), LXIV, 305–322; and Raymond Walters, Jr., "Origin of the Second Bank of the United States," *Journal of Political Economy* (June, 1945), LIII, 115–131.

Apart from those books and articles treating banks directly, there are a number of valuable monographs which explore important economic and political aspects of the Jacksonian era. Two general economic accounts are noteworthy: Douglass C. North, *Economic Growth in the United States, 1790–1860* (New York, 1961) and Stuart Bruchey, *The Roots of American Economic Growth* (New York, 1965). Important interpretations of the meaning and significance of the period can be found in Marvin Meyers, *The Jacksonian Persuasion* (Stanford, 1957); Louis Hartz, *The Liberal Tradition in America* (New York, 1955); John William Ward, *Andrew Jackson: Symbol for an Age* (New York, 1955); and Frederick Jackson Turner, *The Rise of the New West* (New York, 1906), and *The United States, 1830–50* (New York, 1935).

Other studies of particular value include: George R. Taylor, *The Transportation Revolution, 1815–1860* (New York, 1951); Nathan Miller, *The Enterprise of a Free People* (New York, 1962); Walter Hugins, *Jacksonian Democracy and the Working Class* (Stanford, 1960); Joseph Dorfman, *The Economic Mind in American Civilization,* II, (New York, 1946); Whitney R. Cross, *The Burned Over*

District (Ithaca, 1950); Clement Eaton, *The Growth of Southern Civilization* (New York, 1961); Walter B. Smith and Arthur H. Cole, *Fluctuations in American Business 1790–1860* (Cambridge, 1935); Reginald C. McGrane, *The Panic of 1837* (Chicago, 1924); Peter J. Coleman, *The Transformation of Rhode Island 1790–1860*, (Providence, Rhode Island, 1963); Murray N. Rothbard, *The Panic of 1819* (New York, 1962); William W. Freehling, *Prelude to Civil War: The Nullification Controversy in South Carolina* (New York, 1966); Leonard D. White, *The Jacksonians* (New York, 1954) and Alexis de Tocqueville, *Democracy in America* (New York, 1954). A work published after the completion of the manuscript of this book is Jean Alexander Wilburn's *Biddle's Bank: The Crucial Years* (New York, 1967).

No bibliography would be complete without mention of Arthur M. Schlesinger Jr.'s *The Age of Jackson* (Boston, 1946), a brilliant work whose appearance after World War II set off a new round of discussion and investigation into the era of Andrew Jackson.

Index